HELPING MR PATERSON

Pamela Ropner

1982
CHATTO & WINDUS
LONDON

Published by
Chatto & Windus Ltd
40 William IV Street
London WC2N 4DF

Clarke, Irwin & Co Ltd
Toronto

British Library Cataloguing in Publication Data
Ropner, Pamela
Helping Mr Paterson
I. Title
823'.914[J]   PZ7

ISBN 0 7011 2605 1

Typeset by Inforum Ltd, Portsmouth
Printed in Great Britain by
Mansell (Bookbinders) Ltd., Witham, Essex

For Marni

 I

My name is William Seaward. Yes, *the* William Seaward. I must say right at the beginning that I never expected to be famous – and not just here in Britain but all over the world. I never expected to be asked to write my life story, or to become a Fellow of so many august institutions. I never expected to be so rich as to be able to live a life of total freedom, but then, as Mr Paterson would say, you can never be certain of anything.

I mention Mr Paterson straight away because he has, as you will see, an enormous part to play in my story. Without him none of it would have happened. I owe him everything and hope that he will know how I feel. For above all things Mr Paterson understood about freedom.

So I must take you back some fifteen years to Northburgh, the East Coast seaside town where I lived with my two sisters and my mother, and where I first met Mr Paterson.

I am, as you must know by now, an accomplished photographer. But I wasn't always so skilful. No, indeed rather the reverse; but if I have a quality, it is my willingness to learn from others. So, right at the beginning of that summer holidays I went to an exhibition of old country photographs at the local art gallery. These chroniclers of the past have a great deal to teach the amateur photographer and this exhibition was no exception, being depressingly good. I wandered from picture to picture, enjoying the dream-like harvest scenes, the old carts piled high with sheaves, the arched necks of the plough horses, and the village church veiled in an autumn mist. Not really so long ago, yet remote and unfamiliar as a history lesson. There was one study that particularly struck me: the portrait of a fisherman with a

1

wicker basket on his back standing amid skeins of hanging nets. There was something in the intensity of his gaze and in the kind rugged face that was very moving and made me realise the inadequacy of my own efforts. But, I thought, subjects like that did not grow on trees, not in Northburgh anyway. I sighed and turned away, and it was then that I first set eyes on Mr Paterson.

Of course I didn't know his name then, but when I tell you that I saw a man standing at the far end of the gallery dressed in a long white robe of some thick material with a great necklace of what looked like sea shells round his neck, you will understand why I edged nearer to have a closer look. He was very tall – over six feet I'd say, because he was taller than me, and he was very thin, a fact the trailing robe could not disguise. The dark hair that fell below his shoulders was plentifully streaked with grey. He had a pale, fierce, hawk-like face and was staring with a fixed, even awesome, concentration at the photograph in front of him. It was a nostalgic study of a reaper, gaunt as Father Time, in a field of blowing wheat.

I don't know what came over me then. I was not usually so bold, but I felt impelled to speak to this man. I would never get such a chance again, and he was obviously interested in photography, so the chances were that he would be sympathetic to my request.

'Excuse me,' I began hesitantly. 'I wonder if you would mind . . .'

He paid absolutely no attention and continued to stare straight ahead. Perhaps he hadn't heard me. I would have to try again.

'I wonder if you would think it very impertinent of me if I asked you to pose for a photograph?'

I was looking anxiously at him when he turned his gaze full on me. A look of such intensity that it had the physical impact of a blow. I stepped back in spite of myself.

2

'I'm sorry. I didn't mean . . .' I felt I had to apologise, to explain myself, but he cut me short.

'Do you not know that to photograph a person is to steal his soul?' His voice, harsh and whispery, carried to all corners of the gallery. I was acutely conscious of a stir, and someone laughed.

'I didn't think anyone believed that nowadays,' I said.

'I believe it,' he said, as if that was the final word on the subject. Then he turned away from me and walked straight out of the gallery, his robe making a curious rustling sound on the polished wood. The other visitors watched him go with a kind of awe, and I was aware of an acute disappointment, sharp as anything I have ever experienced.

'Hard luck, mate,' a middle-aged man said. He must have heard the whole thing.

'He'd have made a wonderful subject,' I replied.

'Don't just give up, lad. You'll probably see him again. He's not exactly the kind of chap you can miss in a hurry.'

When I think of it, that really is a very good description of Mr Paterson, but I must stick to my story and not digress. I must get down every last detail of what happened to us in that strange and magical summer that was to change all our lives.

I walked back home from the exhibition in a thoughtful mood. It was beginning to rain and a cold wind blew off the sea. I glanced up every side street hoping to catch a glimpse of the man in the gallery, but there was no sign of him. Perhaps I would never know who he was, where he came from. I was filled with inexplicable sadness at an opportunity vanished for ever. I hardly noticed that I was almost home.

Our house was a solid Edwardian villa standing in dignified isolation some hundred yards beyond the boundaries of the town. It was not a pretty house, but had the supreme advantage of an unequalled view of the beach and the sea beyond. We could watch the sea's every mood in warmth and safety from our large, ill-painted windows. There was no garden, only a few scrubby bushes. The sea was our perspective; we had no need of anything else. My father had bought the house some years before as a place we could call our own during his Army wanderings and as an insurance against the future. Which was just as well because shortly afterwards he was killed in Northern Ireland. So there was only Mother and me and my two sisters, Rosalind, who was thirteen, and Miranda, who was eight. She was called Minnie for short because she was so small. As you can tell by our names, our mother has always been extremely fond of Shakespeare.

I opened the garden gate, which was peeling from the harsh salt of the wind, and heard the familiar sound of Ros practising her violin. A fact which gave me no pleasure. It was so long since she had played a proper tune. It was just the same phrases obsessively repeated. Questions posed but never answered. For Ros thought only of the coming audition for the Music School and how she must give a flawless performance on that portentous occasion. An admirable ambition, but difficult to live with.

Minnie was in the living-room, face downwards on the rug, reading, her hands over her ears as usual. She looked up when I came in.

'Did anything exciting happen to you, William?'

I didn't know what Minnie expected of life, but I hoped it would not turn out to be a disappointment. She always looked for excitement in the most ordinary things, which I suppose was a good thing in a way. Usually I had nothing to say, because exciting things very

4

rarely happened to me. This time, however, I did not answer her immediately. She jumped to her feet.

'Come on, William, tell me.' Her large dark eyes were shining. Minnie's eyes were the only large thing about her. I unslung my camera from my shoulder and laid it down carefully on the table. My camera was old, but quite good. In any case it was the only one I had.

'I don't know if this will come up to your exacting standards,' I said slowly.

She seized me in exasperated rage. I felt her fierce little fingers grip my arms most painfully. She was surprisingly strong for someone so small.

'Leave off,' I said crossly.

'*Please*, William, *please*.' Minnie was desperate.

So I told her about the man in the gallery, and as I spoke I realised with a shock how clearly I could see him standing there in his white robe with the necklace of sea shells.

'How fantastic,' breathed Minnie. 'He sounds like a prophet or something. What's a prophet doing in Northburgh?'

What indeed? I thought, and upstairs the plaintive notes of the violin echoed the question in my mind.

'I don't suppose we'll ever see him again,' I said to calm my small sister down.

'We will, we *will*!' cried Minnie. 'I can feel it. This is only the beginning of something marvellous.'

And, as usual, she turned out to be right.

 2

The next day was a Saturday, which was nice as it meant that Mum was able to be at home, in the afternoon. She worked in the local bookshop to supplement Dad's pension, and they closed early at weekends. What was not so nice was the fact that she had invited Mrs Muriel Brewster to tea.

'What on earth did you have to do that for?' I asked crossly. I had intended to spend the rest of the day sorting my photographs into some kind of order. Mum looked depressed and apologetic.

'I know, William. I feel awful, particularly as you cooked such a nice lunch and everything. But it *is* my turn, you know. I've owed Mrs Brewster an invitation for ages and ages.'

She made it sound like a bill that had to be paid.

'Mrs Brewster's not a friend,' I protested. 'She's an interfering know-all.'

'Don't go on, dear,' Mum pleaded. She's not very tall, and has large dark eyes like Minnie's. It's impossible to be annoyed with her for more than an instant. But I really meant what I said.

'Mrs Muriel Brewster is a bore.' I spoke more harshly than I intended, but Ros's incessant practising was getting on my nerves, and it was too wet to go out to photograph anything.

'But she was very kind when Daddy died. She helped me a lot then, and she knows absolutely everyone,' said Mum. And there it rested, although it still seemed to me a very poor reason to ask anyone to tea.

I spent the afternoon tidying a few things in my room, but found I could settle to nothing so it was almost a relief when, promptly at four o'clock, Mrs Brewster drove up in her brand new Range Rover. Mrs Brewster did not have a country estate, but she liked to imply that it was possible if things had been different or if Mr Brewster, a gentle, likeable man whose one preoccupation was the local U.F.O. Society, had more push, as his wife was wont to complain. She had plenty of push for both of them,

6

being a Local Councillor, President of the Women's Institute and Honorary Secretary of the Archaeological Society. No event or social occasion in Northburgh was complete without her. In fact, the pages of the local press would have been positively naked without her large, dominating presence. I steeled myself to welcome her politely into the house and she gave me a gracious smile.

We had tea in the unnaturally-tidy living room. Mum had made an effort with sandwiches and a fruit cake, which Minnie handed round in an unusually subdued way. Ros was silent and moody, fiddling with her long hair, making it plain that she was annoyed to be parted from her violin, even for a short time. But Mrs Brewster did not seem to notice.

'You are so lucky to have such a talented family, Mrs Seaward.' She was in a good mood and had evidently enjoyed the cake. Turning to me she asked, 'Still snapping away, William?' Her eyes were cold and narrow above her smiling, lipsticked mouth.

'I enjoy taking photographs,' I said, heavily emphasising the word.

'Such a nice hobby,' she purred. 'And you, Rosalind dear, still keen on the fiddle?'

I thought Ros was going to say something we'd all regret, but she merely nodded and I saw a flicker of relief on Mum's face. Mrs Brewster rattled on. 'Good, good, we all need something extra in life to help keep up standards. Change and decay all around, that's what I say. It's an endless struggle, as I know to my cost.'

'But surely everything in Northburgh is just as it was?' said Mum.

Mrs Brewster sighed and laid down her cup. 'My dear, I wish it were true.' Mrs Brewster could be very condescending. 'Even the people have changed, and not for the better, no, indeed not. All this freaking in and out or whatever they call it. Drugs and dreadful music. Why, only yesterday I saw a weird-looking man wandering about with absolutely nothing to do. Sponging on the State, I'll be bound.'

I felt a sudden prickle of excitement. I tried to control my voice. 'In what way weird?'

'Oh, you know the sort of thing. Dressed in a long robe with a chain and wild hair that ought to see a pair of scissors. He came right up to me in the street. I was quite nervous. He was so tall, and I'm not exactly small myself.' She paused, deprecatingly.

'What did he do?' Mum was really interested, and there was an amused light in her eyes.

'Nothing at all. That was the unnerving thing. He just stood staring at me. I flatter myself that I'm broad-minded and understand these kind of people. So I asked him if he wanted to give me a flower, you know how these hippies do.'

'But that was ages ago,' interrupted Ros. 'They don't do that now. There are no more flower children.'

Mrs Brewster ignored this remark, although she did not immediately continue.

'Please, Mrs Brewster,' I said, 'tell us what happened.' Something in my tone impressed her.

'He was quite rude. I won't say exactly how, but he was rude. He said something about not giving a daughter of the earth to the unworthy and a good deal more in that kind of vein.' Mrs Brewster flushed at what was obviously an embarrassing memory.

'I'm sure he was perfectly harmless,' Mum said sooth-ingly, trying not to smile. Mrs Brewster snapped shut her expensive bag with a decisive click like a door closing.

'I intend to find out who the man is, and what he's doing here. You can't be too careful these days, so watch out, children. Don't be out late at night. We don't want

8

anything unpleasant. Not here in Northburgh.'

As she spoke, a sharp gust of wind struck the window as if coldly emphasising her words.

'I expect he's quite harmless,' I said, echoing Mum.

'We shall see,' retorted Mrs Brewster, and I felt a wave of sympathy for poor Mr Brewster in his endless search for a world empty of his wife's dominating presence.

Later that evening we discussed what Mrs Brewster had said.

'I feel sorry for anyone Mrs B's got her knife into,' said Mum.

'I think we should warn the poor man,' said Minnie.

Ros was standing by the window looking out at the beach. Her evening practice had not gone well and she was restless and unhappy. She hadn't spoken for a long time. Everyone said she was a pretty girl, although it's difficult to tell about one's sister. She had a sad, musician's face and long hair and she was quite tall for her age. As I looked at her I became aware that she was not staring into space as usual, but focusing intently on something far below on the sands.

'What are you looking at, Ros?'

'It's that man,' she answered. 'I don't think he's realised about the tide. We'll have to warn him.'

'What man?'

I got up, but Minnie was ahead of me, pressing her nose to the glass.

'It's him,' she breathed. 'It must be him. What can he be doing?'

I reached the window and we all looked down on the sands below. There was a rock some hundred yards out to sea, where we often used to rest while swimming. It was accessible when the tide was low, but at high tide it was completely covered. Upon this rock, staring out to sea, motionless as if carved from white marble, sat the man I had seen the day before in the gallery. As we watched, the tide swirled in more strongly to cream round the base of the rock, which was by now totally cut off.

'Doesn't he realise he'll have to swim for it if he doesn't come ashore?' Ros said.

'We'd better shout,' Minnie suggested.

'I doubt if he'll hear us from here,' Ros pointed out, 'but we'd better try.'

Together we wrenched up the window and yelled in unison as loudly as we could. 'The tide's coming in! Get off the rock!'

But if he heard us at all he gave no sign.

'I'll have to go down to him,' cried Mum. There was no one else on the beach. It had been far too wet and, although it was momentarily clear, the clouds still hung heavy with rain. But she had spoken to an empty room. We were already racing out into the garden down the narrow path that led to the beach.

At the water's edge all three of us stood shouting at the watcher on the rock, which was now partially submerged.

'Either he can't hear us or he doesn't understand,' said Ros, looking at me.

There was nothing for it. I stripped off shoes, shirt and trousers, and in my torn yellow underpants plunged into the exceedingly cold water. As there hadn't been a real summer to warm the seas around Northburgh, the temperature was even colder than usual. I struck out boldly for the rock, swimming hard against the incoming current. The wind had whipped up the waves so they heaved and jumped at me. I was not sorry to reach the rock and to seize the trailing edge of the stranger's robe. The jerk of the material on his shoulders brought him at last to life and he looked down at me – a penetrating gaze

10

devoid of surprise at my dishevelled appearance.

'Come on,' I cried. 'You can't stay there.' I had to shout above the increasing noise of the water.

'It comes to something when a man cannot sit in peace without being disturbed by a hysterical youth,' he replied coldly.

I was pretty annoyed at this. 'All right, drown if you want to.' I shook the wet hair out of my eyes.

'I don't think that's amongst my most pressing desires,' he said in his curious whispery voice that sounded over the sea wind. Then without warning he rose to his feet and gathering the dripping robe about his thin person he stepped off the rock. The water was quite deep, but he was so tall that, standing upright, his shoulders were above it. The ends of his long hair floated like an elderly mermaid's. A careless wave broke over his head and he emerged spluttering, teeth chattering. I launched myself into the water behind him and gripped his arm. He made no effort at all to swim, but somehow, with a combination of luck and my good swimming, we progressed slowly but steadily to the shore where Minnie jumped up and down with excitement. Ros was smiling in an amused way. I must say I thought they could have done more to help.

We emerged from the disrespectful waves with some dignity, I like to think. My rescued companion gave an excellent imitation of Neptune, which was rather impressive, as he adjusted his shell necklace and a belt embroidered with white shells and tossed back his dripping hair.

'I wish you to know that I am not ungrateful for your kind attention,' he said.

At this Minnie giggled. 'But what were you doing out there?'

'Waiting of course,' he said, as if that had been completely obvious.

'What for?' asked Ros.

11

'For the voice of the sea to speak to me.'

'And did it?' Minnie will believe absolutely anything.

There was a long, painful silence. A gull swooped overhead calling mournfully like a lost soul, and I saw an expression of great sadness on the man's face.

'No, it didn't,' he said, gathering up his robe. 'But there is always another time.' And he walked away.

We watched him go in silence. When he was some distance away he turned suddenly and looked back at us. His voice came faintly on the wind from the sea.

'You must listen for the old world.'

We stared after him until he was out of sight and we were all wondering what he meant as we walked back home.

Mum was waiting anxiously for us.

'Well done, William. You did awfully well. I saw it all from the window.'

'He wasn't a bit grateful,' said Minnie. 'He didn't even say a proper thank you.'

'I think he did . . . in a way,' said Ros, but she didn't tell us what she meant.

'We must find out who he is and every single thing about him.' Minnie was still bubbling with excitement. 'He's the oddest person I've ever met.'

'Any finding out will have to be tomorrow,' said Mum firmly. 'It's the first Saturday of the holidays and I've really pushed the boat out for supper.'

She needn't have worried. This was an event of such rarity that nothing would have induced us to be out that night. Mum doesn't cook often, not really cook I mean, but when she does the gods themselves would not be disappointed.

Much later I was up in my room, restless and unable to sleep, and it wasn't just because I'd eaten too much roast chicken and chocolate gateau but because the events of the day kept returning to my mind. I had sorted out all my photographs into heaps and altered the ones that hung on the wall. But there was something lacking, especially in the portraits of many of my school friends, and people in the village who had obliged with a sitting. The carefully-lit faces were there all right, old and young, plain and pretty, smiling or serious, yet something was missing. Something essential. With a shock of recognition I realised what it was. My friend in the gallery need have no fear. None of them was in any danger, for I had totally failed to steal away their souls.

 3

I slept in the next morning so I was still in my dressing-gown when Mum and Minnie returned from church. Ros was out at an extra music lesson. Minnie was in a high state of excitement.

'We've found out who he is and all about him.'

For a moment I could not follow her, being only half awake. Minnie was maddened by my blank expression.

'The man on the rock, stupid. The man you rescued.'

'What about him?' I tried to conceal the leap of interest in my heart.

'His name is Mr Paterson and he lives in the old fisherman's cottage near the cliffs,' said Minnie, full of triumph.

'If you can call it live,' added Mum quietly.

'What do you mean?'

'Apparently he came here only a short time ago and moved into the empty cottage.'

'But it's practically a ruin,' I protested.

'Exactly. It must be the most uncomfortable place. No one seems to know anything about him. Who he is or

13

where he comes from, nor why he's dressed as he is. The vicar was in a conversational mood,' Mum added, by way of explanation.

'I wish he wouldn't call me sprite,' moaned Minnie in disgust. 'If there's one thing I can't stand it's that.'

I laughed sympathetically, but of course the vicar was quite right. With her dark eyes in her pointed face, framed by her curls, Minnie looked every bit a sprite, although a tough one when she was angry.

'Perhaps we should do something to help him,' said Mum doubtfully. 'But people don't always want any.'

'We could go and see,' I said.

'Oh, yes, yes,' shouted Minnie. I wished she wouldn't, so early in the morning.

'You don't want to intrude on his privacy.' Mum was frowning.

'But we must warn him.'

'About what?'

'If Mr Paterson is living like a tramp in the old cottage, Mrs Muriel Brewster will get to hear of it and she'll never allow a thing like that. Never, never, never.'

I glanced at Mum. I think the same thought had occurred to her.

'We'll go this afternoon when Ros is back.'

Ros returned from her music lesson in a strange mood. She said practically nothing over lunch and we gathered that Miss Jessop had not been pleased with her progress.

'You mustn't set your heart on this place at the music school,' said Mum gently. 'It's not the end of the world if you don't get in.'

The violence of Ros's reaction surprised even us, who were used to her artistic outbursts. She flung down her knife and fork and ran from the room crying that no one understood her.

14

'I suppose it wasn't really much of a lunch,' sighed Mum as we were clearing away the remnants on Ros's plate. But she looked sad and worried just the same. However, by the middle of the afternoon Ros seemed better and Mum thought it would do us good to get out for a bit, so we decided that the time had come to go and visit Mr Paterson.

The cottage where Mr Paterson had chosen to live was at the far end of the sands, tucked away beneath the shadow of the cliff. We knew it well and when younger had often played in the small rooms, long ago vacated by a local fisherman because of the constant danger from the encroaching sea and probable falls of rock from the cliff face. Yet the place had the undoubted charm of seclusion, being reachable only by a rather uncomfortable walk across slippery rocks and fallen cliff boulders. We picked our way carefully over them.

As we approached the cottage we heard the sound of a loud hammering. Whatever Mr Paterson was doing, it was certainly not sitting about. He had his back to us and was hitting briskly with a large wooden mallet at a wide plank of driftwood. He was so absorbed in his task that he did not hear or see us until we were right beside him. He straightened up and looked rather sternly at us, but there was no surprise in his eyes.

'We've come to help you, Mr Paterson,' said Minnie confidently, but then she would.

'I am not aware that I require help,' replied Mr Paterson.

We didn't know what to say next. To fill in the awkward silence Ros said, 'What are you doing?'

'Hammering a nail into a piece of wood.'

'What for?' I asked.

He sighed as if we were the stupidest creatures in the world. 'I'm making a raft.'

'Why do you want a raft?'

'After yesterday's episode I should have thought that was obvious,' he said shortly.

The thought of Mr Paterson balanced on a home-made raft was not something that appealed to any of us, me especially.

'Don't you think that's rather dangerous?' I said.

'And it would be awfully difficult to swim in your robe,' said Ros.

'If you fell in,' explained Minnie.

He smiled then, a quick sweet fleeting smile that lit the deep-set eyes. Then he turned and went into the derelict cottage.

'I don't think he wants us here,' said Ros.

'I'm sure he doesn't,' I agreed. 'Perhaps we'd better go.'

'We can't. We haven't given him the warning about Mrs Brewster,' hissed Minnie. We stood, uncertain what to do next.

I don't know what we would have decided, but at that moment Mr Paterson came to the broken doorway and beckoned us. All his movements were slow and unhurried, which gave his every gesture a curious intensity that could not be ignored. He beckoned and so we went without question. It was always to be like that with Mr Paterson.

Minnie was the first inside the old cottage so that I heard her gasp of astonished delight before I saw what so entranced her. The room in which we now stood was as I remembered it. Very decayed and damp with an uneven stone floor, cold to the feet. Yet there my memory ended, for it was transformed. Every inch of the peeling walls was covered with a fantastic mosaic of shells of every size and colour, and from every region of the world. Large shells, horned like a crab, shells of white like the purest sand, mother-of-pearl, a delicate Venus' ear, flat shells

16

with scalloped edges like white ferns, shells twisted and fluted and mottled like the sea on a windy day, creamy whelks, mussels, mysterious blue like the ocean deeps, shells like the abandoned horns of sea unicorns, yellow and pink like a tropic morning, huge shells like the cradle of a young sea monster, or tiny and delicate, transparent as a butterfly's wing. We stood, all three of us, in awed silence. We had never seen anything like it.

'But how did you manage it?' I asked at last.

'Superglue is one of two products of this industrial society that I permit myself to use. So decorative a purpose seemed justification enough,' explained Mr Paterson. There was no answer to that.

'I think it's the most beautiful thing I ever saw,' whispered Minnie, and that summed things up perfectly. Ros and I murmured our agreement.

'Then I hope you'll stay to tea,' said Mr Paterson, surprisingly.

'That would be lovely,' said Ros quietly, as if she did not find the idea at all unlikely.

'Then have the goodness to collect some sticks for a fire,' answered Mr Paterson. Needless to say Minnie was first through the door.

Tea with Mr Paterson was not an impossibility, but not exactly a pleasure. The second product of the industrial society that he permitted himself to use turned out to be firelighters and soon our collected sticks were blazing in the tiny fireplace. On this he placed an old kettle.

'What about cups?' asked Minnie. She didn't know the meaning of reticence.

'Follow me,' said Mr Paterson, beckoning meaningfully. Together they went into the only other room, which was as yet undecorated as far as I could see. I heard Minnie give another of her theatrical gasps and they emerged bearing the tea things. I saw what she had meant. These were no ordinary cups, but shells cut down to manageable size, to some of which Mr Paterson had attached handles of driftwood with crude twine. The shell cups balanced perilously on saucers made from scallops, and the plates were scallops too, a little chipped here and there, but serviceable enough. Nevertheless I was relieved to see that the tea pot was a real tea pot, even if it lacked a lid.

Tea was another matter altogether. From a container shell Mr Paterson tipped into the tea pot a large amount of some dried greenish-looking substance onto which he poured boiling water from the kettle. There was an awful smell, a cross between seaweed and old socks, and I wished I wasn't so thirsty.

'I make my own tea from a mixture of herbs and dried seaweed,' Mr Paterson told us with some pride. 'So much better for the body.'

And on the principle that anything revolting is better for the body, the tea was certainly effective. I had never tasted anything so disgusting. Somehow I managed to drink it down, as did the others, although Minnie made some awful faces. In fact, we drank several cups, but turned down an offer of boiled eggs.

'A pity,' murmured Mr Paterson. 'They're quite fresh – most of them anyway.' I thought Ros was going to laugh, but she managed to control herself.

The tea eventually came to an end, but it had taken quite a time because the shell cups retained the heat and you had to keep laying them down to avoid burning your fingers. And as fast as we emptied them, Mr Paterson filled them up again.

'I am glad,' he said suddenly, 'to be able to repay you in some small measure for your kindness of yesterday.'

'That's all right, Mr Paterson,' I muttered, but I was pleased all the same.

18

A silence fell. The little fire crackled and burnt a bluish flame. Outside the sea hissed and surged, and rattled the pebble beach. It was so peaceful that it might have been the beginning of time.

'Mr Paterson, what did you mean about listening to the old world?' asked Ros, just like that. It was clever of her to choose exactly the right moment for such a question. For several minutes Mr Paterson didn't speak. Then he leaned forward, staring into the dying fire, the flames reflected on his carved, ivory face.

'So much noise and strife. We can no longer hear our Mother's voice,' he replied, sadly.

We waited. There was more to come. We knew that because he turned his intense gaze on us, and I noticed for the first time that his eyes were a curious dark watery green like a seapool. He went on in his strange, harsh voice.

'We are all Children of the earth, yet we cannot hear our Mother's voice. Our Father the sea calls to us, but we have forgotten how to listen.'

This sounded very sad and impressive, but what did it mean? Mr Paterson apparently read my thoughts, for his eyes were on me.

'You saw those photographs at the exhibition. In those days, before machines came, people still heard the voices of the earth and sea. You could see it in their eyes.' The cracked voice rose excitedly. 'That is what we have all lost. The ability to hear the voices of the old world, and I intend to get it back, even if it takes me the rest of my life.'

'But how?' I was caught up in the excitement.

'Yes, how, how?' echoed the other two.

'By returning to my origins.' Mr Paterson was on his feet, his face alight with a fervour that was frightening. 'By casting off all trappings of modern society and returning to the way we were meant to live before the

19

machines came. Only then will I hear again the old voices. I am a Child of the earth. We are all Children of the earth. All —' He broke off suddenly and turned away. 'I don't expect you to understand,' he said rather sadly. 'Most people think I'm off my head.'

I didn't know what to say, but Ros did. 'We do understand, Mr Paterson, and I think what you are doing is wonderful.' She really meant what she said.

'We'll help, really we will,' cried Minnie.

But Ros had not finished. 'Teach me to listen, Mr Paterson.'

He shook his head. 'I can't do that,' he said shortly. I saw the disappointment in Ros's eyes.

'Why not?'

'We have to find our own gods in our own way,' he said and without another word strode out of the cottage, where he stood absolutely still looking out to sea. We wondered if we should go home.

'We still haven't warned him about Mrs Brewster,' Minnie reminded us as we made our way over the sand to where Mr Paterson was standing. I took on the responsibility. He listened politely to what I had to say about Mrs Brewster. I tried to put things as forcefully as I could.

'Mrs Brewster hates people like you. She'll try to get you out. She's a Local Councillor. She has the power.' I was insistent, but Mr Paterson seemed quite unmoved.

'The forces of evil are all about us, but should they come I shall be ready. When I begin to hear the voices of the earth and sea they will tell me what to do about Mrs Brewster. Have no fear.' He sounded so confident that there was nothing for it but to leave, having thanked him for the tea and trying not to trip over the half-completed raft.

On the way back across the beach Minnie said, 'He didn't even ask our names.' She sounded put out.

'Is he mad, do you think?' I asked Ros. For a long time she didn't reply.

'I don't know. He may be, but I liked what he said about the old world.'

I wondered what she was thinking, but feared to ask. Ros has always hated her private thoughts to be disturbed.

'I wonder what he does for money,' said Minnie. 'He can't have much.'

'No, but everybody has to have some,' said Ros. 'The eggs must have cost something, and the hammer and nails.'

The mention of them worried us. 'I just hope,' said Ros, 'that he never finishes that raft.'

Late that night Mum woke me up by switching on my light. Her eyes were large with alarm and she was very pale.

'What is it?' I asked, sitting up.

'Minnie isn't in her room. I thought I heard her, so I got up and looked. She wasn't there. The bed's all pulled back, but she's not there.' She tried to keep the fear from her voice.

'Don't worry, I'll find her,' I said. I was already out of bed, searching for my dressing-gown and slippers. Even as I spoke, an idea flashed into my mind about where Minnie might be.

'Put out the light,' I said quickly. Mum did as she was told and I ran to the window. Looking out, I felt a great surge of relief.

Below on the sands stood Minnie, a small distant figure in a white nightgown standing almost opposite Mr Paterson's rock, holding out her hands towards the sea.

'She's down there,' I said.

'What on earth can she be doing?' Mum was bewildered, dizzy with relief.

'I'll find out and bring her back.'

The night wind was cold against my face as I left the house and hurried down the path to the beach. The roar of the sea had a hollow sound and windy clouds trailed across the moon. I was beginning to be angry and wish I was back in bed.

'Minnie,' I yelled. She seemed at first not to hear me. 'Minnie!' I shouted again, breaking into a run. As I approached she turned towards me and I saw in the uneasy light the shine of a tear on her cheek. She ran to me and burying her face in my dressing-gown began to cry in earnest. I gripped her thin shoulders, frail like a bird's body, and pulled her away to look into her face.

'What are you doing, Minnie?'

'I was listening for the voice of the sea, doing what Mr Paterson said. We are all Children of the earth and the sea was our Father. I've been listening and listening, and I didn't hear anything. Not anything.' A sob choked her voice, then she wailed, 'I'm frozen. Let's go home. I'm sorry if I frightened you, William.'

I took her cold hand in mind. 'It's O.K., Min,' I said. I really am very fond of her, even though she is sometimes so annoying.

Over a cup of cocoa Mum asked, 'What did you expect to hear down there, Minnie?'

'Just things,' she said vaguely.

'What things?'

Minnie slammed down her cup, her small face flushed. 'It's a secret,' she said angrily. 'And I say people oughtn't to be asked about secrets.'

'And I say the same people with secrets ought to run off to bed,' responded Mum firmly.

Long after Minnie was asleep Mum and I sat talking over the events of the night, which had made her very sad.

'It's times like this, William,' she murmured, 'when I miss your father most of all. He'd tell us what to do about Minnie. And Ros,' she added, almost as an afterthought.

'I do my best,' I said in a hurt way. Mum was immediately concerned.

'You do everything for us, William. I don't know how we would get on without you. But you have your own life to lead, and your own worries, I dare say, and now this. I don't want Minnie to get too involved with Mr Paterson, whoever he is. I'd say we had enough to worry about without him. If only your father . . .' Her voice faded and I thought she was going to cry.

'We all miss Dad,' I said gently, and as I said that I was thinking about Mr Paterson.

'Minnie was so young when he died,' said Mum, 'she can't remember that much.'

But I thought later that night, just before I fell asleep, that perhaps Minnie missed Dad most of all.

 4

The next time we saw Mr Paterson was two days later. Mum had gone to talk to Miss Jessop about Ros's music. Ros had gone to see a friend and I had gone to meet Minnie after her riding lesson at the local stables. The ride had just returned and Minnie couldn't wait to dismount from her fat grey pony, to which she gave only the most cursory of pats before running over to me.

'Really, Miranda,' called the riding mistress, 'you must try to show Greylag a little more appreciation.'

'Sorry,' called Minnie in an off-hand way, without looking back. I sometimes think that Minnie doesn't like ponies any more than I do. She just pretends because she thinks it's the thing to do.

'Let's go back through the park,' Minnie suggested, and she ran on ahead of me so that I had to hurry to catch her up.

The park was at the far end of the town. A large, dull patch of grass, with a miniature golf course and putting-green, a few tennis courts, a croquet lawn, the park was not exceptional. Its saving grace was a very extensive boating lake, a paradise for small boys with model ships and for old folk and young lovers in the numbers of ancient but serviceable boats you could row about for ages for not too much money. In fact, we all learnt to row there; so much safer than the sea, Mum said, though I thought it a bit tame at the time.

As we approached the place, I had the feeling that all was not as usual. For one thing there was much more noise and a good deal of laughter, sudden shrieks, dogs barking and the inevitable baby yelling its head off.

'What's going on?' I said and we broke into a run round the corner, through the main gate, until we could survey the whole park and the wide lake, shining in the rare July sun.

'Oh no,' gasped Minnie, in horror, as well she might.

For there in the middle of the lake, balanced precariously but with an affecting dignity, on the home-made raft, was Mr Paterson. He had procured a long pole from somewhere and was sculling along amid a crowd of jostling boats like Moses amid a crowd of ignorant Egyptians. The wind caught at his white robe and blew his long hair. The shell necklace was over his shoulder. He looked both marvellous and ridiculous, proud yet strangely pitiful. I could have wished he had been more skilful with the pole, but alas, he seemed quite unable to control his frail craft and bumped and knocked the cluster of small boats. Soon the peaceful scene was rent with angry shouts. Minnie and I ran to the edge of the lake.

24

'Mr Paterson,' we shouted, over and over again. 'Come off the lake. Please come off!' But to all our entreaties he gave no answer, just an ill-advised wave of the pole, which knocked a portly, red-faced man right into the bottom of his boat. Then, like a swan breaking free from a vulgar crowd of ducks, he propelled himself with a certain grace into the very centre of the pond.

The angry shouting continued and the park attendants appeared. The boat hirer kept bellowing, 'Come in, your time's up!' but Mr Paterson obviously did not understand what he meant and paid absolutely no attention. So it might have gone on. Then Minnie gasped.

'Look, William. Look what's happening to his raft.'

She was right. The home-made raft, tested beyond its limits, was slowly coming apart. Mr Paterson's sandalled feet were already in the wet.

'Come ashore. You're sinking!' I yelled. Surely even a prophet must notice when he's up to his knees in water. The end came quite suddenly. The raft collapsed and Mr Paterson was thrown into the water and, still clinging to his pole, sank beneath the surface. This time the pond was too deep even for his height. With a feeling of *déjà vu* I stripped off and for the second time that week rescued Mr Paterson from a watery grave.

This time it was no picnic. As Ros had foreseen, the wet robe was a great hazard and Mr Paterson was exceedingly heavy. At one point I thought I was going to fail. Nevertheless, to the unwanted cheers of the onlookers, I managed to drag him to the shore, where he lay with closed eyes, scarcely breathing.

Minnie let out a shout of dismay. 'You're not dead, are you, Mr Paterson?' she cried, kneeling beside him.

It seemed an age before the green eyes flickered open. 'No, child, I am not dead.' A reasonable enough answer in the circumstances.

He levered himself painfully into a sitting position, and water from his sodden hair ran unchecked down his face. I could see that he was shivering.

'I see I am once more in your debt.'

I shook my head, sending out a shower of drops. I was shivering too. 'Come on, you must get out of that wet robe as soon as possible.'

As I spoke I realised that we were almost completely encircled by a crowd both curious and angry. Someone said it oughtn't to be allowed and there was a jibe about not walking on the water if you couldn't swim. The red-faced man was complaining loudly to the boat hirer and a small boy was sobbing. The park attendants pushed themselves to the front and went on a good deal about unauthorised craft on the lake and demanded to know Mr Paterson's name and address. These he gave them with great dignity.

'Adrian Paterson, the Fisherman's Cottage, The Beach, Northburgh.'

'Are you having me on, or something?' demanded one of the attendants. 'No one lives there now.'

'I do,' said Mr Paterson, and so saying, he stood up rather shakily, surveying his critics. Beneath his stern gaze they fell oddly silent.

'Let's get him out of here before he catches cold,' suggested Minnie.

I could see she was right, as usual; the white robe was muddy and still dripping, and although it was July and sunny, there was a nasty chill breeze off the sea.

'Come home with us, Mr Paterson. We'll get you dry somehow.'

'The wind will do that,' he replied calmly. Nevertheless there was a grateful expression in his eyes and he made no protest when Minnie took his hand and began to lead him away.

'You'll be hearing more about this,' the park attendant warned, and as if released from a spell the others started up again. But Mr Paterson ignored them all and we walked away, the three of us, straight out of the park gates on to the road home.

Now I am not easily embarrassed, but walking back with Mr Paterson took quite a little doing. As we went, passers-by turned to look in astonishment, and not a little amusement. The soaking robe clung to his thin body, making him look stranger and more outlandish than ever, even to a public long used to hippies and drop-outs. There was, however, something different about Mr Paterson which was difficult to define, and Minnie did not seem to notice anything unusual. She clung to his hand in a very determined way as if he were a trophy that she had somehow captured in a war.

We were half way down the street when I saw to my dismay that a white Range Rover was parked a little further down. Someone was sitting in the driver's seat, watching us. I tried not to look, but somehow could not resist a glance. I stared straight into Mrs Muriel Brewster's hard, scornful eyes. She said nothing as we passed, but I saw that she was gripping the steering wheel very tightly until her knuckles showed white. Clearly she had not forgotten her first encounter with Mr Paterson. And she was not a woman who forgave.

We reached our garden gate at last. Here Mr Paterson hesitated.

'I don't wish to trouble your good mother,' he said, but Minnie wouldn't hear of anything else.

'Don't be silly, Mr Paterson,' she said, and undid the catch with a decisive click. As we went down the path we could hear Ros playing upstairs, very fast and brilliant, without any breaks or repetitions. Mr Paterson stopped

27

short to listen to her and I saw him frown, but he said nothing. Once inside we called for Mum.

She came out of the kitchen and showed a commendable lack of dismay when she saw Mr Paterson dripping all over the hall floor.

'Oh dear,' she said. 'You must get dry or you'll catch your death.'

'He will come when he is ready and not before,' reproved Mr Paterson.

'I wouldn't care to risk that,' Mum said with a smile, and she hustled Mr Paterson into the downstairs cloakroom, from which he duly emerged swathed in a long towel which still did not reach his bony sandalled feet. He looked exceedingly uncomfortable.

Mum then did something very unexpected. She ran upstairs and returned with something dark draped over her arms. I saw to my amazement that it was my father's regimental cloak, which she had hung in her wardrobe since his death. She draped it gently round Mr Paterson's shoulders. My father had been a tall man too, so the cloak fitted exactly, sweeping down to the floor. Even dressed only in a towel he looked splendid.

'My dear lady, I couldn't possibly . . .' began Mr Paterson, but Mum held her finger to her lips.

'Not another word. It suits you wonderfully and my husband would have been glad to know that his cloak had kept someone warm. It's a cold world outside, Mr Paterson.'

'It is indeed,' he replied solemnly.

While Mr Paterson's robe was drying out on the line we had tea. Ros had stopped practising and came to join us.

'So you are a musician,' said Mr Paterson, looking keenly at her, adding, beneath his breath, 'I should have guessed.'

Over tea we really began to know Mr Paterson, or at least as far as it was ever possible. He explained to my mother his theories about the old world and listening for the voices. She seemed rather impressed.

'There's a lot in what you say, Mr Paterson. But will you ever be able to prove it?'

He smiled such a mysterious, withdrawn smile that I wondered what he was going to say next, but his reply was totally unexpected.

'I'm afraid I don't know your names. If we are to become friends, that would seem the first essential.'

So we told him we were William, Rosalind and Miranda Seaward – 'Because I'm so fond of Shakespeare,' explained Mum.

'But I'm really called Minnie because I'm so small,' Minnie said coyly. She can be so awful at times.

Mr Paterson turned a stern gaze on her upturned face. 'I shall not call you Minnie. If the great bard of Avon considered the name Miranda suitable for one of his creative images, who are you to distort it?'

I thought Mum was going to laugh, but she merely poured another cup of tea, saying, 'Tell us more about yourself, Mr Paterson. How have you come to be here?'

For a long time Mr Paterson did not answer. Then he said, in a far-away voice, almost a whisper, 'I was born in the Andaman Isles in the Pacific Ocean. My father was a colonial civil servant. Not an important one. More of a clerk really.'

'What a wonderful place to grow up,' said Mum.

'I didn't, more's the pity,' sighed Mr Paterson. 'My father got into financial trouble. We came home from there when I was a small child. Otherwise I would have learnt to swim.'

We laughed at that. 'And you never went back?'

'No.' He fell silent for a moment before continuing.

29

'My father never got over leaving there. I think his heart was broken. He used to sit for ages by my bed telling me about the emerald seas and the dolphins and how at sunset the horizon was turned to gold like the frontiers of paradise.'

'How wonderful,' breathed Minnie.

'And he didn't bring back anything to remind him of the place he loved except the robe and necklace and a most wonderful collection of shells, which he would sit holding to his ear, listening to the voices of the deep.'

'What did they say?' asked Minnie.

'I don't know. He never said. My mother used to get angry and talk about getting out and earning his living, but he wasn't very good at that, I'm afraid. When he died he didn't leave anything except debts and the seashells. And then there was no time for any listening or any thinking for me. I had to pay off his debts and keep my mother going to the end. I went to work in a bank, but I never made much of it. No interest, you see. They can always tell.' He bowed his head as if that long-ago burden was still with him.

'What did you do then?' asked Minnie impatiently.

'Gently, Minnie, gently,' said Mum.

'I worked until everything was paid off, and until my mother died. Then, in the next few years, I discovered I could save just enough money to follow my own star. Not much, mark you, but enough. So I took my shells in a suitcase, put on the robe that Father had brought back with him, and the necklace, and walked out into the night.' He raised his head then and I saw that his eyes were burning. 'I'm free now, you see, to return to my origins. I want to hear the old world speak. I want to know the old gods, and walk this beautiful earth in their company.'

'I'm sure you will, one day,' said Mum encouragingly.

30

'We'll help you, Mr Paterson,' whispered Minnie. 'And then it's bound to be all right.'

We had finished tea and Ros went outside to see if the robe was dry. The wind had done its work; the rough woven material was good as new. Mr Paterson changed back into it in the cloakroom and came out holding the cloak.

'Please keep it,' said Mum. 'My husband would have been so pleased. But I'll just have to change the buttons. They don't like you to wear them if you aren't in the regiment.'

Mr Paterson finally took his leave of us, and from the living-room window we watched him walk across the sands in his dark cloak. He looked like a pilgrim journeying to an unknown land. Wherever it was that he wanted to reach, I hoped very much that he would get there in the end.

5

For two or three days we did not see much of our new friend. He spent several hours sitting on the rock, but usually very early in the morning, to avoid attracting attention, I suppose. I saw him once when, jerking awake after a nightmare, I went to the window to look out. It was just after dawn and a light mist veiled the calm sea, which was as well, for there, silent and upright on the rock, sat Mr Paterson. The mist swirled round his still figure, giving him a ghostly look, as if he had no more substance than a dream. I wondered if he might vanish away altogether. But he must have taken account of the tide because there were no more episodes of that nature. Late the next evening I saw him again on the rock, but this time he was attracting the amused attention of some

31

walkers, who pointed and laughed in a rather rude way. But if he heard them he gave no sign, and only continued to stare at the darkening horizon.

'I wonder,' said Minnie a few days later, 'if the voice of the sea has spoken to him yet.'

'Doesn't look like it,' said Mum. 'Poor Mr Paterson. What if it never does? He'll be there for ever,' she added, half under her breath.

But that very afternoon I was in my dark room at the top of the attic stairs when I heard Minnie's rapid foot-steps on the uncarpeted stairs. I had been looking with dissatisfaction at some undistinguished images floating in a sea of Hypofixative, so I was not, for once, too annoyed to have an interruption. I just had time to put away anything that might be exposed by the light when Minnie burst in. Even in the half dark I could tell that she was very excited. The words came tumbling out in such disarray that I couldn't make out what she was saying. Something about Mr Paterson and a hill and the uni-verse.

'I don't get you,' I said. 'Start again.'

Minnie sighed. 'I met Mr Paterson this afternoon and he said he wanted us to go with him to Northburgh Hill tonight.'

'What on earth for?'

'He said that if you want to return to your origins you must try and hear the voice of the universe, and the hill is the best place to do it. I expect he's tired of waiting for the sea.'

I doubted that myself. 'I don't think we should go.'

'Oh, but we must,' cried Minnie. 'We simply must. He's counting on us. He asked me to tell Ros to bring her violin.'

'Good heavens, and have you?'

Minnie's face clouded. 'Yes, William, I have and she's

not very keen. Because of the damp, she told me. She said her violin isn't a Stradivarius, but it's the only one she's got.'

'I can see her point, and I think we shouldn't go. I'm not sure that it's right to encourage people in mad ideas.'

'But we must help Mr Paterson. We *must*. He hasn't got anyone else,' pleaded Minnie. And on and on she went until in the end I gave in.

'All right then, we'll give it a try if you insist. But just this once though.'

It was well after ten that night before we started our climb of Northburgh Hill with Mr Paterson. Mum hadn't been at all keen on letting us go and even though Minnie had eventually managed to persuade her she had insisted on pullovers and sandwiches and thermos flasks of hot coffee. We were equipped like a polar expedition, which made it all the more difficult to keep up with Mr Paterson, who strode on ahead without looking back.

'Returning to your origins is very tiring,' grumbled Minnie.

'Well, you were the one who wanted to come,' I said crossly. She had no answer to that.

Ros brought up the rear, carrying her violin in its case. She kept glancing anxiously skywards in case it rained. She needn't have worried. It was a lovely night. Above us the stars glittered and there was a moon in this summer firmament. The sea below shone with splintered light. I could smell the night dew on the grass as we walked, and suddenly it didn't really seem so odd at all that Mr Paterson should expect to hear the voices of the universe. That was his strength. He could make the unreasonable seem entirely reasonable, which I suppose is why we followed him.

Just before reaching the crest of the hill Mr Paterson

halted, holding up an imperious hand.

'Here, I think, is a suitable place,' he said.

The hill was grassy smooth, except for a few scattered boulders which would be good to lean against and be out of the night wind.

'That's fine,' I said, glancing back to where the lights of Northburgh were spread like animals' eyes in the dark, watching us.

Mr Paterson leaned against a large boulder and turned his face up to the sky.

'Can't we have some coffee before we begin?' asked Ros, who seemed tired and rather cross. I expect she was still worried about her violin.

'You must try to raise your mind to a higher plane, Rosalind,' said Mr Paterson, reprovingly.

I decided to ignore this last remark and got on with pouring out the coffee and handing round the sandwiches. This may not have raised our minds, but it certainly raised all our spirits, and in spite of his superior approach Mr Paterson seemed to enjoy our bizarre picnic, especially the sandwiches. Then, the small meal over, we settled down to the serious business of listening.

And now the enchantment of the night had us in its spell. Not silent, but full of little carrying sounds. A wandering owl, far away sheep, the distant hiss of the sea, and above, the immense mysterious sky, remote yet not really out of reach, a part of us all in a way. I was beginning to enjoy myself.

'Will you play for us, Rosalind?' asked Mr Paterson. Ros looked startled, but she must have expected to be asked. Yet still she hesitated and said something about the dampness of the night air and not knowing what to play. I couldn't blame her, but Mr Paterson would have none of it.

'The violin is the voice of dreams,' he said. We weren't

sure what that meant, but it sounded nice. So Ros snapped open the black case and took out her violin and tucked it carefully beneath her chin. She had a good deal of tuning to do because of the night air, and all the time Mr Paterson was silent. But at last she was ready.

'What shall I play?'

'What you feel,' said Mr Paterson quietly.

Ros began to play a difficult measured piece, Bach, I think. She played well, with no mistakes, but it was oddly cold and remote from our attentive ears. Even I could tell that. Mr Paterson turned and looked at her.

'Is that really how you feel, Rosalind?' he asked.

She didn't answer, but stopped playing. The notes died away and she stood uncertainly, the violin beneath her chin, the bow held motionless in her outstretched hand. Then she smiled and nodded. She drew the bow slowly across the strings, producing a long, delicate singing note that made me shiver. It was a different sound altogether. Then she launched into a familiar sparkling song: Ariel's song from *The Tempest*, a magical evocation of perfect freedom.

'Merrily, merrily shall I live now, under the blossom that hangs on the bough,' sang the violin. As the words echoed in my enchanted mind Ros played all the verses, and as the light, carefree notes finally died away I realised that perhaps only Ros of all of us really understood about Mr Paterson. It was a new Ros who stood before us. She was before a door that had so long been closed to her but now was open, beckoning her into a bright and brilliant land.

'Thank you, Rosalind,' said Mr Paterson, and I could tell by the way he spoke that he was very pleased with my sister.

Ros didn't play again and we settled down for a bit more listening. I don't know what Mr Paterson expected, but none of us heard a thing. We were all hoping so much for him and we sat in silence for ages. Minnie began to wriggle and complain.

'Returning to our origins is very boring,' she whispered noisily, so that Mr Paterson must have heard, but he said nothing.

'I want to go home now,' she said, but more loudly this time.

'Don't, Minnie, you'll spoil everything,' Ros snapped.

'You're a beast,' retorted Minnie.

Mr Paterson walked away from us then and I can't say I blamed him. He walked almost to the top of the hill and stood looking upwards. The wind wrapped the robe against his body as he held out his arms to the unresponsive stars. I've never wanted anything so much in my life as I did that night. Please, I said inside myself to whoever might be listening, please answer him.

'If the stars had voices,' said Minnie suddenly. 'I think they'd be cold and tinkly like a chandelier in the wind.' She can be very unexpected.

Ros said nothing but stroked the violin which she held cradled in her arms like a child.

The silence around us deepened and I became aware then of something strange and new. The stars were like dew on an invisible web that bound us each to the other. Here on the hill we were together, the universe and ourselves.

I motioned to the others to follow Mr Paterson to the brow of the hill and we crept behind him as silently as we could. But he heard us and turned round. Even in the uncertain light I could read the disappointment in his eyes.

'They will not speak tonight,' he said in a low voice.

'Perhaps this is the wrong place,' I said gently.

'I wanted to believe, I really did,' whispered Minnie.

I don't know what would have happened next if at that

very moment we hadn't heard a distant murmur of voices over the crest of the hill. Far away at first, then growing ever nearer. It was very eerie. I could feel myself grow cold.

'Whatever is it?' whispered Minnie. She crept close beside me and put her freezing hand in mine. Ros clutched her violin case tightly to her. Only Mr Paterson seemed unafraid. He moved away from us and held up his hand. I couldn't see him very well, but the excitement was in every inch of his tall figure.

'They have heard my call. I will go and meet them.' And as he spoke the voices grew even louder. There was some laughter in the night air, and a dreadful doubt flashed through my mind. But Mr Paterson started forward eagerly, sweeping me aside with his imperious hand. He went over the crest of the hill, arms outstretched to meet his long-awaited destiny. He stood for a moment outlined against the night sky. The wind blew at the white robe and he looked impressively old and awe-inspiring.

The voices ceased abruptly. I heard a wild cry, an answering murmur and a sob of fear. I dodged behind a boulder where I could see directly what was happening. It was no use meeting a difficulty head on until one saw what it was. I motioned to Ros and Minnie to stay back, and I stared out into the moonlight. A group of people were advancing up the hill. I couldn't see who they were in the flickering dark, nor how many. But at the sight of Mr Paterson they stopped dead and stood in a confused huddle. There was a tense silence. Then without warning a man in a duffle coat came forward, his hand held palm upwards, arm bent at the elbow. He walked very slowly and cautiously, stopping some yards from Mr Paterson.

'Welcome, O traveller from another planet. We come in peace to greet you.'

The man's dim face and voice were vaguely familiar, even though he intoned the words in a strange singing voice as they do in science fiction films. I realised with a shock of dismay what had happened. What with the dark, the late hour, the atmosphere of belief, perhaps even the distant sound of Ros playing, everything had conspired to fire the over-active imaginations of the Northburgh and District U.F.O. watchers on one of their searches for evidence of other, more perfect worlds. As I hesitated, uncertain what to do, the voices broke into an eerie chanting, echoing their leader's words.

'Welcome, O alien from another world. We welcome you . . .'

I couldn't allow this to go on, so I dashed over the brow of the hill, followed by my sisters, and we waited behind Mr Paterson who stood tall and forbidding, just like an alien in fact. In the bewildered silence that followed as the voices died away, the watchers on the hill understood that their precious dream was not to be realised, not that night at least. As the moon appeared from behind a single trailing cloud we all saw ourselves for what we were. Ordinary mortals, if one could ever term Mr Paterson ordinary. Then, suddenly, Mr Paterson laughed. Throwing back his prophet's head he let out a roar of sheer delight, blowing away the shreds of his disappointment in a gale of unexpected mirth. Then Ros laughed, then Minnie, and soon we were all overcome, drowning the shouts of 'What a shame,' and 'It's only the old hippie,' and other less complimentary descriptions of Mr Paterson. I'm afraid people who have been made a fool of are seldom at their best, although soon they too broke into laughter. All but one man, who stood in silence at the back of the merry throng. He was Mr Henry Brewster, who looked as if his world had broken, like the laughter, into a million fragments.

We sobered up enough at last to walk down the hill, all atmosphere having gone from the night. Everyone was looking closely at Mr Paterson with an interest I found alarming. Many of the U.F.O. watchers were from some distance away and hadn't heard about him. I realised as I looked at their eager questioning faces that his fame was about to spread much further than Northburgh, and I wondered, as we walked, if this was altogether a good thing.

At the town centre we parted politely from our companions and set off for home. At the gate Mr Paterson said goodbye to us, but nothing was said about another meeting, nor any remark made about the events of the evening. This time he only looked straight at Ros.

'*Merrily, merrily shall I live now,*' he said quietly.

'*Under the blossom that hangs on the bough,*' she responded, and I saw that she was smiling.

Mr Paterson walked away with his head held high. He looked as if he hadn't a care in the world, even if the universe hadn't, as yet, said a single word.

 6

The following morning the door bell rang just after we had finished a latish breakfast.

'Who on earth can that be?' sighed Mum. 'I thought we'd had enough excitement for a bit.' And as she said this she glanced at Ros and Minnie's pale faces. She had the morning off from the bookshop, so we had all had breakfast together for once.

'I'll go,' I said, and a moment or two later opened the door to a slight, bespectacled man in a brown polo neck and a worn leather jacket.

'Mr William Seaward?' he asked. I was taken aback.

People don't usually call me that.

'Yes.'

He held out a small neat hand. 'Martin Parker, reporter, from the *Northburgh News*.'

'What do you want?' But before I knew what was happening he had somehow got past me.

'May I come in, Mr Seaward? I'd like to see your sisters too, if you don't mind.' He was heading for the kitchen.

'Wait a minute,' I cried, but I was too late. Mr Parker was already shaking my mother's hand and looking closely at Ros and Minnie, still both in their dressing-gowns.

'Just a minute, Mr Parker,' I said angrily. 'I didn't say you could come straight in.' But he had already got out his notebook and a small black tape recorder, which he laid on the table.

'You're a reporter, aren't you?' Minnie's eyes were bright with excitement.

'We have nothing to say to the press. We're just an ordinary family minding our own business,' said Mum, catching my disapproval.

Mr Parker twiddled his pencil before asking, 'What can you tell me about the man in the white robe?' There was a silence, so he continued, 'I've heard all about last night, you know. That's why I'm here.'

'I see,' I said. No one else spoke. Mum shook her head suspiciously.

Mr Parker broke the silence again. 'Come on, kids, give me a break. Nothing ever happens in this dump and now we have a prophet in our midst and talk of aliens and travellers from a far planet and all that. I can't just pretend it hasn't happened.'

'Why did you call him a prophet?' asked Mum.

'That's what he is, isn't it?'

'But a prophet of what?'

'That,' said Mr Parker, snapping on his recorder, 'is what I hope you are going to tell me.'

I suppose we should have shown Mr Parker the door there and then, but he looked rather depressed and down at heel in his shabby jacket, as if he knew that the main thoroughfare of Northburgh would be his only Fleet Street.

'If you put that machine away we'll tell you a little of what we heard,' I said.

'You're a champ, boy,' said Mr Parker, and he began to look slightly cheerful.

We didn't say much really, just that we hadn't known Mr Paterson long and that he was looking for a new or an old way of living, depending on which way you looked at things. I admitted to the park rescue though.

'Yes, I heard about that too.' Mr Parker chuckled.

Ros said nothing, but Minnie kept trying to interrupt, although I wouldn't let her. I didn't give a long interview, and after offering him a cup of coffee – which he accepted and swallowed almost in one gulp – we sent Mr Parker on his way. He looked positively cheerful by the time he left us.

'I hope I didn't say too much,' I said uncertainly. I know now, as I think I suspected then, that a reporter can enlarge the slenderest of tales into a full-blown production, given half a chance, and we had certainly given Martin Parker that chance.

We spent a quiet day recovering from our night's adventure on the hill. After lunch Mum went into Northburgh to do her afternoon's work. When she returned that evening she had an evening paper with her, and she was looking very worried.

THE PROPHET OF NORTHBURGH, screamed the headline, and beneath there was a blurred photograph of Mr Paterson. He was sitting on the rock, so the photograph must have been taken by a holidaymaker. *What is his secret and why have the Seaward family befriended this Man of Mystery?* There was a good deal more in this vein, including a rather inaccurate Moment of Terror report by one of the U.F.O. watchers. We read on and on in increasing dismay.

'Mr Paterson will be furious when he finds out,' said Minnie, voicing all our thoughts.

'Perhaps he won't read it,' said Mum, but I knew she did not believe what she said.

'We'll have to warn him,' I said. 'People will be starting to take an interest and they'll go to his cottage. They'll take away his privacy . . .'

The idea was too dreadful to contemplate. We had destroyed Mr Paterson's treasured freedom.

'They won't stop at papers. There's local TV and radio.' Ros rubbed salt into the wound.

'Some things are just a passing wonder. They'll soon lose interest once they find that he's only a poor old crank,' said Mum comfortingly.

'He's not a crank, Mummy,' shouted Ros. She's usually so quiet, it was a shock to hear her shout like that. 'He knows a kind of truth. I don't exactly know what it is, but I intend to find out.' She spoke with great feeling, and her beautiful pale face was flushed.

'It's all right, dear, don't get excited,' soothed Mum. 'But whatever it is, I think Mr Paterson deserves a warning as quickly as you can get to him.'

We hurried over the sands towards the rocks and the fisherman's cottage. The beach was more crowded than usual and one or two people watched us go with a more than cursory interest. As we reached the place we saw that our friend was not inside his uncomfortable house, but sitting on the shingle beach looking out to sea.

42

'You bring bad tidings. I can feel it,' he said, not turning his head.

'It's – it's something in the paper. We didn't mean any harm . . .' I began.

'In that one sentence you encapsulate the troubles of the world,' he answered, and held out his hand for the paper, which rustled in the wind of the approaching tide.

We watched apprehensively as he read the whole page. For a moment there was no reaction. Then he tossed the paper to the wind, which seized on the thin pages and whirled them away to the water's edge where the accusing front page floated for an instant before sinking beneath the surface.

'I would have you know, my friends,' he said quietly, 'that I am not so easily deflected from my purpose.'

'But they'll come and pester you. What about your freedom, your privacy?'

'No, no, William. All from within. All from within,' he said, rising to his feet. 'The old gods have been mocked. We must propitiate them.'

'What's that mean?' asked Minnie eagerly, on the scent of something new.

'We must make a sacrifice.'

'I'll soon find a goat or a sheep.' Minnie had a tendency to be blood-thirsty.

'Not a goat or a sheep,' answered Mr Paterson firmly.

'But when and how?' Minnie persisted.

'No more questions, Miranda.' Even Mr Paterson found her exhausting, but still she did not give up.

'Where and when?'

'Tomorrow afternoon at the stone circle at Wythy. At three o'clock.'

And that was all he would say to our repeated questions. I could see that we would have to go in the end.

*

'I'm worried about you spending so much time with Mr Paterson,' Mum said to me later that evening. 'I don't think it's altogether advisable.'

'You've been talking to Mrs Brewster,' I said.

'She's been talking to me, you mean,' sighed Mum. 'She's cross because I won't go on her jaunt. I'm far too busy for that kind of thing and anyway I hate crowds.'

'What jaunt?' I was curious to know.

'You know how proud she is of the Archaeological Society. Well, they're going to hire a bus, and someone from the National Trust is coming to give a lecture on ancient land marks in the area.'

A sudden anxiety seized me. 'Does this lecture include the Wythy stones?'

Mum shrugged. 'I suppose it must. Mrs B said something about it, but I'm afraid I wasn't really paying attention.'

'So you've no idea what time or where this jaunt is going?'

'None at all,' said Mum, adding as an afterthought, 'I suppose it will be in the afternoon. The trip wasn't due to begin until two o'clock.' She looked at me curiously. 'Why do you want to know all this, William? Surely you have no intention of going?'

So I told her.

'You must stop him,' Mum cried in alarm.

'I don't know if I can.'

'But surely after last night's incident he won't want to get muddled up with another society, particularly with Mrs Brewster in charge.'

'I'll do my best,' I said doubtfully, thinking that it was probably easier for Canute to turn back the tide than for me to change Mr Paterson's mind.

'Why does Mrs Brewster hate Mr Paterson so much, do you think?' I asked.

44

'I'm not absolutely sure,' said Mum thoughtfully. 'She was going on and on about her husband being humiliated in front of all the U.F.O. watchers. But it's not really that, is it?'

I thought for a moment, before Mum answered her own question. 'People who follow a different path from the rest of us sometimes make the rest of us feel uneasy, insecure if you like; a natural reaction of the herd against the one stray animal. Mrs Brewster belongs to the herd.'

'You make it sound very grim.'

Mum's eyes were bright with intensity. 'I never used to think in our Army days. There just wasn't time. But if there's one thing I've learnt in the bookshop, it's that we need these kind of people almost as much as we need food and shelter. The poets, the music makers, the thinkers and the prophets. Without them, life is nothing.'

'And the photographers?' I asked. She touched my hand.

'Even the photographers, William.'

'I'm not getting on too well with it these days,' I admitted.

Mum looked at me sympathetically. 'I don't wonder at all, what with 'A' levels, changing schools when Daddy died and everything. But there's still time. Rome wasn't built in a day.'

My mother is a marvellous woman; she made no prisons for her children.

'Try to persuade him not to go anywhere near the stones, William. A sacrifice can't be legal in this day and age.'

And we both laughed. You couldn't always help it with Mr Paterson.

Of course I ought to have gone that very evening to warn our friend, but I didn't. And it's no use saying the gods prevented me or anything like that. I just didn't feel like going and there was something good on television that evening. I did go the next morning, but he was nowhere to be seen, and call and call as I might there was no reply. So I tried not to think about anything going wrong all the way to our appointed meeting place. I said nothing about my anxiety to the other two.

7

The standing stones of Wythy are not exactly a rival to Stonehenge. Nevertheless they are quite interesting. Situated some three miles outside Northburgh, in the very centre of a large patch of flat stony grass, they are preserved by the National Trust as a permanent witness to our ancient past.

The place is seldom without one or two people wandering about, and that afternoon was no exception. There were a few bored school children on an organised holiday outing with their teacher, and two motor cyclists in woolly hats, who were larking around on an oblong fallen stone in the middle of the circle.

'I wouldn't do that if I were you,' warned the teacher. 'It's the sacrificial stone and seen some grim history, I'll be bound.'

The woolly hats grinned and said something rude not quite under their breath. There was no one else in sight, so Ros, Minnie and I sat down thankfully on the grass to recover from our long hot walk. The air seemed very close and thundery, and behind us a bank of heavy cloud was beginning to darken the sky.

'I hope Mr Paterson won't be too long, or I'll fall asleep,' said Minnie. She lay back and closed her eyes against the glare of the sun. I was about to do the same when I saw the woolly hats staring over my shoulder in distinct alarm.

'Would you look at that?' they gasped, infecting the rest of the visitors with their alarm. I glanced round and saw Mr Paterson striding towards us over the grass, tall and upright, carrying an old sack over his shoulder, his white robe stark against the darkening sky.

'A druid,' gasped the children. They were standing very close together, as if to protect each other; I must say I couldn't blame them.

'Must be some kind of solstice or something,' someone murmured. No one laughed. I could tell by the way they looked that they were none too sure from which century the advancing figure had so timely stepped.

There was dead silence until Mr Paterson reached us, when he said, 'I'm glad to see you are not late, my friends.'

Minnie sat up. 'What's that in your sack?' Her eyes were wide.

There was no answer from Mr Paterson.

'Is it a knife for the sacrifice?' She has a very clear voice, and the visitors, who had begun to relax, stiffened again. Unconsciously they gathered into an apprehensive group at the far end of the circle, patently torn between curiosity and unease. There was no one else in sight and I began to relax; perhaps the uncertain weather had deterred Mrs Brewster and her archaeological companions.

Mr Paterson advanced confidently towards the sacrificial stone. We followed and stood watching doubtfully as he circled the stone several times, muttering some strange incantation under his breath. I hoped the gods were not listening. When he unslung his sack there was a silence you could have cut with a knife, if you know what I mean. To my intense relief there were no sheep's entrails, nothing unpleasant like that, but infinitely more surprising. Out of his sack Mr Paterson took a battered frying pan, a carton of eggs, a small bottle of oil and his only other concession to the industrial society: a packet of firelighters. He also had a bundle of driftwood and a box of matches. At the sight of this strange collection the watchers cheered up. They moved forward for a better view. As Mr Paterson meticulously piled up the fire-lighters and sticks on the sacrificial stone, so the crowd drew nearer.

At this point I felt I had to intervene. 'You can't do that. I'm sure it's not allowed.'

'The gods won't like that. It may be blasphemy,' agreed Ros.

'And it's not even a proper sacrifice,' moaned Minnie, as Mr Paterson struck a match. The firelighter blazed and caught the tinder-dry driftwood.

'There's nothing wrong with sacrificing an egg. Anything else would have been too difficult. The gods are infinitely understanding,' Mr Paterson assured us, reaching for the frying pan. I had to admire his nerve, but I think Minnie would have been happier with a real live virgin.

But at that very moment his luck ran out. In the corner of my eye I saw a large green bus draw up at the edge of the field to disgorge itself of some thirty people, just as Mr Paterson, with another unintelligible incantation, poured a little oil into the pan. He opened the carton, which Minnie held in her eager hands, and broke four of the eggs into the pan. Then he held the pan over the fire, and immediately the eggs and oil made a delicious frying sound, bubbling and hissing. There was ironic applause from the woolly hats and they sniffed the air apprecia-tively. The school children were giggling, reaching for their cameras, just as the bus load approached the stone

48

circle. My heart sank as I spotted Mrs Brewster, in a green anorak with binoculars slung round her capable and capacious shoulders and carrying a blackthorn stick, striding purposefully at the head of the group. The gods cannot have been on our side that day or they would not have allowed the Northburgh Archaeological Society to visit the stones at the very instant Mr Paterson was making his sacrifice. Or it may have been that they simply did not care for fried eggs. For a sudden, horrified moment the newcomers stood staring at the curious scene which met their eyes. The eggs fried merrily and the surface of the sacrificial stone was beginning to darken with the fire. The two boys grinned, unable to believe their luck. Mrs Brewster, her face very flushed, and not just from the heat of the afternoon, advanced like an avenging spirit.

'Desecration! Heathen vandal!' she stormed, but Mr Paterson paid no heed. Gently lifting the pan off the flames and holding out the cooked eggs, he raised his face to the sky in a kind of dedication. He looked happy; whatever else was going to happen, at least he had made his sacrifice. Mrs Brewster gave a gasp of rage. The woolly hats sidled up, trying unsuccessfully to keep straight faces.

'Please, Mister,' one of them spluttered, 'me and my mate is hungry. We forgot the caviar.' And they both fell about laughing.

With a single swipe of her stick, Mrs Brewster swept the dying fire off the stone onto the grass, where the ashes lay smouldering. She was speaking rapidly in a loud voice, quoting bye-laws that had been infringed, Trust rules that were broken – the list was endless. The sun had gone in and every moment the sky grew darker. The onlookers began to shift uneasily as Mrs Brewster beckoned forward a man in a tweed suit.

'This is Mr Blake of the National Trust.'

'I'll have to look into the rules, Mrs Brewster,' he protested, rather feebly.

'You must do your duty,' she snapped, glaring so fiercely at Mr Paterson I thought she might burn him with her eyes. He merely folded his arms and waited, smiling his inward smile. I rather admired him then, in spite of the trouble he had caused us all.

Mr Blake advanced and cleared his throat. 'It is my duty,' he began nervously, 'to warn you that the National Trust does not permit . . .'

The audience was tense with expectation, but in the end it was cheated. At last the gods stirred themselves to action, bringing the extraordinary scene to an abrupt end. There was a terrific clap of thunder and a silver sword of lightning struck the field only a hundred yards away. A torrent of heavy rain was released from the disapproving heavens. We were soaked to the skin in seconds and, as one, we all made a bolt for the road and the shelter of the bus and parked cars. We pelted over the grass at a great rate, Mr Paterson easily out-distancing both Mr Blake and Mrs Brewster. In the centre of the abandoned circle the sacrificed eggs raised their yolks to the falling rain.

But at the road Mr Paterson didn't stop, but crossed it and set off at a rapid pace towards the sea. We watched him until he was out of sight, and I saw a look of relief on Mr Blake's harrassed face that he did not as yet have to pronounce upon the rules of the National Trust on the subject of sacrifices.

'Your friend will be receiving a summons,' warned Mrs Brewster grimly as she stepped back into the bus; the rain had ruined her hairstyle and her make-up had run, but there was in her eyes a look of determination, hard as the standing stones. The bus drove off as soon as the Society

50

were all aboard, leaving us forlornly in the rain.

By now those of us left behind were extremely wet, but the school party was in good spirits, having had an entertainment beyond any of their wildest expectations.

'You can never tell what's going to happen next in this wonderful world,' the school teacher said, adding admiringly, 'Your Druid friend's a real original, isn't he.'

I nodded vaguely, though I was relieved that Mr Paterson was not there to hear. Meanwhile, the show being over, the woolly hats roared off on their motor bikes, and we began the long trail home. I was feeling extremely worried and, as you can imagine, didn't feel at all like talking.

'You're very quiet, William,' said Minnie. She glanced up at me and there was a curious expression in her dark eyes.

'I was thinking,' I said defensively.

'What about?' asked Ros.

'About knowing that beastly Mrs Brewster and her archaeological society were coming to the stones,' said Minnie.

I stopped dead. I was so angry I couldn't speak, but of course Minnie was right.

'I was listening at the door. I heard what Mummy told you.'

I seized Minnie by the shoulders. I felt like shaking the life out of her, but she broke away from me.

'It's no use getting cross with me, William, when you didn't bother to go and warn Mr Paterson,' she cried.

'I don't know which one of you is the worst.' Ros strode on angrily ahead.

'Why didn't you go youself, Minnie, why?' I was genuinely puzzled.

Ros heard me and turned back. Her look was full of cold contempt and even Minnie seemed embarrassed.

51

'I wanted Mrs Brewster to come here with her society and then Mr Paterson would show them that he can do anything. He could have made the gods strike down his enemies. It might have been marvellous.' She sounded most disappointed.

'Minnie,' cried Ros, in a shocked voice. 'You are a savage. Civilisation hasn't even begun to touch you.'

'I'm not frightened of you,' muttered Minnie, who had not really understood.

We walked in silence, miserable in the unrelenting rain.

'Mr Paterson must have an affinity with water,' declared Ros wearily, after the first mile or so.

'What will happen to him now?' I ventured anxiously.

'He'll have to appear in court, I suppose, if he really has broken the law.'

'And then what?' I was really alarmed. 'Oh lord, he's in real trouble now and it's all my fault.'

Ros didn't answer, but Minnie took my hand quite gently. 'Don't worry, William. Mr Paterson will be quite all right. And he isn't afraid of anyone at all.'

I just hoped that she was right.

Later that evening, when the rain had at last stopped, we saw that Mr Paterson had returned to the rock. He must have been cold because he was wearing Father's cloak. The tide had already turned. I hoped that he was not going to sit in contemplation for too long.

I studied him closely. The odd thing was that although he was motionless he gave the impression of movement, as if he was travelling somewhere in his mind. I imagined him in some vast primeval forest, holding up his arms to the munificent gods. Always when I thought of Mr Paterson, strange new images flashed into my mind. Some buried memory of a million years struggling unbidden to the surface, or a vision of the future? I hoped that the gods, if gods there were, would repay his indestructible belief.

 8

From the day of Mr Paterson's sacrifice the summer weather steadily deteriorated. The rain seemed endless. Minnie grew bored and restless. Ros ceased to practise. In a way this was a relief, although Miss Jessop did not think so. She came to see Mum about it one evening. She was a small, bird-like woman in an Indian-style dress which was too young for her. I was the only one downstairs. They forgot all about me in their anxiety to have a discussion.

'Rosalind seems to have lost all interest in her music,' Miss Jessop complained. 'She needs to practise all the time if she is to have a chance of a scholarship, or even give a good performance at the festival concert in September. One never knows who may not be listening.' She was referring to a biannual event in Northburgh's calendar: a small but influential group of concerts and poetry readings very well attended not only by the local community but by people from much further afield, sometimes even from London. Ros had been chosen for a violin concerto with the orchestra of the local comprehensive school where we were all now being educated since our wandering Army days were over.

'Didn't she give any reason for her change of heart?' asked Mum.

Miss Jessop sighed heavily. 'All she said was something about waiting for the old voices to speak, about music being the soul of the earth. Very poetic, I'm sure, but I

don't know what it means, or where she has heard all
that . . .'

'I know,' said Mum shortly.

Miss Jessop looked surprised and pursed her lips.
'Well, if you could have a word with Rosalind, Mrs Seaward, I would be so grateful. I have other pupils, and
time is running short.' She rose to her feet to emphasise
the point.

'It was very nice of you to come, Miss Jessop. I'll speak
to Rosalind. I'm sure everything will be all right.' Mum
tried to sound reassuring.

'I hope so,' said Miss Jessop, but she went away shaking
her head.

Mum did speak to Ros, but it wasn't a success. Ros
listened with a mutinous expression on her face.

'I'm trying to work something out,' was all she would
say.

'Then I only hope it's worth it, whatever it is,' replied
Mum. 'Musical talent is a gift from the gods –'

'I know that,' interrupted Ros. 'Why can't you leave me
alone?' And she made another of her dramatic exits,
slamming the door behind her.

I wasn't getting on any better either. I hadn't even
looked at most of the essays set for the holidays, and my
lack of success at photography depressed me more and
more. There were so many good photographers in the
world. How was I ever going to make my mark? If only I
could take just one fantastic photo which would set me
apart from the rest. A masterpiece of originality that
would launch me fast as a neon flash into a career of fame
and fortune. But I knew that was only a dream. More
than likely I would end up behind a bank counter or
manager of a supermarket and that would be the end of
that.

That evening there was some disturbing news in the

54

paper. A large headline proclaimed *NORTHBURGH PROPHET ON SERIOUS CHARGE* and there followed a brief and not strictly accurate account of the events at the standing stones. Mr Paterson would appear in the Magistrates' Court the following day.

'We must be there,' said Minnie.

'You're too young to go in.'

'I can stand outside and think about him,' she replied defiantly. You couldn't get the better of Minnie.

We hadn't seen Mr Paterson for days and I felt guilty about him. The fisherman's cottage must be horribly damp and uncomfortable in this weather. I hoped he had been eating properly despite leaving his frying pan at the stone circle. Being a prophet wasn't easy, not in this day and age.

The following day we walked into Northburgh. The Magistrates' Court was in the main street, an elegant square flint building of some antiquity with an interior of panelled oak that gave it a dignified and sombre appearance. The rain had cleared, for the moment at least, and the sun was attempting to shine through watery cloud. We got to the court early to wait for Mr Paterson. There was already quite a crowd assembled, and I was just able to get a seat inside by saying I was a friend and had been at the stone circle. Ros and Minnie had to wait outside. There were one or two cases before Mr Paterson's, which the magistrates – briskly chaired by a Colonel Scott – dealt with swiftly and efficiently. Besides the colonel there were two other people on the bench: a Mrs Manley and a Mr Saunders, a fat red-faced man who looked like a butcher.

There was a pause and some whispering in the court. I heard a muffled sound in the street outside as if someone was shouting, and laughter. After a few minutes Mr

Paterson came through the door and walked over to the dock where he remained standing bolt upright. He looked older and thinner, and his robe was torn at the sleeves. But the shell necklace was intact and now he wore a shell-embroidered band around his greying locks. His eyes were without expression. The court, which included Mr Blake and Mrs Brewster, looked at him curiously.

'Your name is Adrian Paterson,' said Colonel Scott. He glanced at a paper before him. 'Of no fixed address.'

'Wrong,' said Mr Paterson sharply.

'But you are Adrian Paterson and you are at present squatting – I'm afraid there's no other word for it – you are squatting in the derelict fisherman's cottage under the cliffs, are you not?'

Mr Paterson chose to ignore this slight. 'My name is Adrian Paterson and I am a Child of the earth.'

This remark caused a minor sensation and the audience leaned forward for a closer look.

The colonel frowned. 'This court is to be taken seriously,' he ordered, continuing in a toneless voice, 'You are Adrian Paterson of no fixed address, and you are charged with causing damage to property of historic interest belonging to the National Trust and with creating a public disturbance. What have you to say? Do you plead guilty or not guilty?'

There was a long silence.

'You are required to answer the charge,' said Colonel Scott, quite politely.

'If it is a crime to use a place for the purpose for which it is built, then it is wrong to pray in an empty church or read a book in a library and I have indeed committed a crime.'

There was a ripple of laughter around the court and I saw Martin Parker scribbling rapidly in his notebook. But Mr Paterson's undoubted logic had upset the magistrates.

'So you plead guilty?'

'Certainly not.'

'But you were present at the stone circle at Wythy on the day in question and you will admit to causing a disturbance there.' There was an edge of irritation in the colonel's voice.

'I will not. I was not responsible for any disturbance. In fact, I would go so far as to say that the assembled company rather enjoyed my peaceful little ceremony.'

'Hear, hear,' shouted someone, and I saw the owner of one of the woolly hats grinning broadly in the front row of the public gallery.

'Silence in court,' intoned the Clerk.

But the colonel was clearly interested. 'So you plead not guilty?'

'I do.'

'Then I think it would be a help to the court if you would explain the reasons behind your actions and indeed why you have chosen to come to Northburgh and – er – live amongst us.'

Mrs Manley nodded in agreement and folded her arms in anticipation of Mr Paterson's reply. There was a tense, expectant silence. I could hear the ticking of the large mahogany clock, but at last the accused began his explanation.

'I did not choose Northburgh,' he said. 'Ancient forces led me here to be at the edge of things. It is – it is not at all easy to explain.' He paused.

'Do go on,' urged the colonel. 'Take all the time you need.'

Mr Paterson looked around him then, as if seeing the sea of faces for the first time. In all his life he can never have been given such a chance, and he seemed suddenly aware that he must grasp it with all the power he could command. He raised his head and the strange, harsh voice filled the crowded room.

'We must listen for the ancient voices. We must show the old gods we have not forgotten them. We are all Children of the earth and we must learn again to hear our Mother's voice and the call of our Father the sea.' He spoke movingly about all that had been lost and might yet be regained. You could have heard a pin drop. He seemed to have the power to reach out to the listening people, even if they did not fully understand all he said. No one moved.

'So I have made my sacrifice,' he told them proudly, 'and the gods will answer me, in their own way. Be assured that —' He paused for a moment, dramatically, before continuing:

> *Not in a green shade does contentment stay,*
> *But in the touch of the apple tree's primeval bark*
> *We find excitement's brilliant way*
> *Into the dark.'*

For several seconds the echo of these words seemed to linger in the stillness, then vanish in a spontaneous burst of applause. I saw Martin Parker smile slightly; he was still scribbling away with great enthusiasm. The colonel adjusted his spectacles.

'Is that all you have to say?'

'That is all.'

The colonel turned to Mrs Manley. 'You wanted to add something?'

'I did indeed,' she replied with unexpected sharpness. 'Mr Paterson, we have heard in this court a great deal of nonsense. I put it to you that you are no more than a layabout and a publicity-seeker, a trouble-maker who is unlawfully occupying condemned premises. What is your answer to that?'

'One of the things I support is freedom of expression,'

said Mr Paterson mildly, but with dignity.

Mrs Manley had not finished. 'I have also heard that you seek to influence the younger generation with your subversive, blasphemous theories. Old gods indeed. I have no doubt that the only "old god" you have any acquaintance with is Bacchus, god of wine!' Mrs Manley was clearly pleased with her classical allusion. Mr Paterson merely smiled, and the audience shifted uneasily in their seats.

'I seek to influence no one. I follow my own star.'

The colonel was beginning to lose patience. 'Yes, yes, we've heard all that once. Now I think it is time we examined the facts of the case.'

There was never any real doubt about the verdict, having heard the evidence given by Mr Blake and by the police sergeant who had investigated the report. All that remained was for the court to pass judgement. Colonel Scott delivered this solemnly. Mr Paterson was bound over to keep the peace. From Mrs Brewster's expression I guessed she would have preferred something a good deal more severe, but she appeared better pleased when, just as Mr Paterson was leaving, someone went up to him and pressed into his hand a long, official-looking envelope. Mr Paterson barely glanced at it, but strode off without a word. Although he had lost his case, he looked a winner all the way.

 9

On the way home we went past Mum's bookshop. We stopped and stared in at the window. We were feeling very dejected. It had taken me some time to push my way out of the crowded courtroom and when at last I found myself once more in the street, there had been no sign of

Ros or Minnie. I had had to hang around for what seemed ages before they appeared, breathless and with long faces. Ros explained where they had been. Apparently, they had followed Mr Paterson when he emerged from the court and, with some difficulty, had managed to catch up with him at the far end of the street. According to Ros, Minnie had pestered him with so many questions that in the end he had told them what had happened in court. Then he showed them the letter. It was an eviction order. Mr Paterson had to be out of the fisherman's cottage within the next fortnight. I remembered Mrs Brewster's look of satisfaction and wondered if that could possibly explain it, but I said nothing. We walked on in silence.

There was no one in the bookshop, so we went inside. This was something Mum usually discouraged, but not this time.

'How did it go?' she asked.

We told her.

'Poor Mr Paterson.'

'What'll he do now?' asked Ros.

'He'll have to leave the cottage, and if has nowhere to go . . .' Mum paused and we contemplated Mr Paterson's bleak future.

All this time Minnie was wandering about the shop looking at the books, admiringly touching the shiny covers and turning the pages of one or two. She became so absorbed that we almost forgot she was there. Mum made us some coffee in the small back room and we joined her there. We were sipping the hot liquid from the pottery mugs when Minnie burst in, her face alight with excitement. She was holding open a large glossy book.

'Careful with that, Minnie dear. It's very expensive,' warned Mum, but Minnie was not to be deterred.

'Look,' she cried. 'Do look!' We crowded round to see

60

what had so intrigued her.

The book was an expensive production called *Denizens of the Sea Shore*, and Minnie held it open at the centre page. There was the most beautiful illustration of many types and varieties of shells. We looked on, uncomprehending. Minnie stamped an impatient finger on the drawing of a large curling shell like a huge whelk, but with a scored, ribbed exterior and a centre of delicate rose-leaf pink. *Triton shell from the Pacific. Believed by the Romans to be Neptune's horn*, it said underneath. We still didn't see the point. Minnie was exasperated.

'The old voices won't answer if all you do is stand and wait for something to happen. You have to call them to let them know you want an answer.'

'Call them?' asked Mum. 'How?'

'With a proper horn, of course,' said Minnie, as if it was the most obvious thing in the world.

'But what's all this got to do with Mr Paterson?' asked Mum, removing the book from Minnie's none too clean hands. There was an expression of triumph on my little sister's face that was most irritating, but I had to know.

'He's got a Triton shell just like in the picture. It's too big to hang on the wall. I saw it in the other room when I was helping with the tea.'

'You never said anything about it before.' I was suspicious.

'I didn't think it was important before,' answered Minnie.

'And so?' said Ros curiously.

Minnie was infuriated by our obtuseness. 'We must go and tell him at once,' she cried.

'Don't you think he's in enough trouble as it is?' said Mum.

'Yes, we don't want to encourage anything else that might go wrong,' I said, backing Mum up.

61

Minnie turned on me, her eyes blazing. 'Can't you see, stupid, that *this* is the message from the gods. Don't you remember after the sacrifice Mr Paterson said you never knew how or when they would answer. Well, they just did, here in this shop. To *me*.' Her voice was full of importance. 'I'm going to tell Mr Paterson whether you like it or not. And if none of you want to come, I'll jolly well go by myself.'

I glanced at Mum, who nodded wearily. There was no stopping Minnie in this mood. Yet I felt uneasy at the prospect of lending any more encouragement to Mr Paterson's fantasies, if fantasies they were. 'OK, OK,' I said. 'But it would be more to the point if we tried to find him a house.'

'I suppose that would be more sensible.' Ros sounded reluctant. I knew she found the attraction of Mr Paterson's ideas very strong.

'I'll go without you both then,' Minnie threatened again.

'Wait a moment, all of you,' Mum intervened in a thoughtful voice. 'What Minnie says about the Triton shell being Neptune's horn may have some relevance after all. Now I think about it I remember reading a book once about the fish-callers of the South Seas. Quite fascinating.'

'Fish-callers?' Ros and I echoed.

Mum nodded. 'Evidently some inhabitants of those islands used to stand on the beach and blow these large shells and the fish would swim into shallow water, more or less sacrificing themselves on the sand. It's an ancient art, though whether mere skill in predicting the pathway of shoals and movement of fish played a part or whether it was something a great deal more mysterious I can't possibly tell you.'

'So you think there's just a chance Mr Paterson might

get an answer from the sea or the old voices, and not necessarily the one he's expecting?' I said.

Mum shook her head. 'Perhaps you shouldn't say anything at all. There's probably nothing in it anyway.'

'But it can't do any harm,' pleaded Ros, and Minnie, seeing she was going to get her way, jumped up and down in anticipation.

We went straight away.

Looking back, I suppose it was a curious decision to tell Mr Paterson about the Triton shell, but that was the effect he had on us all. We desperately wanted to believe in him. We wanted to see his theories succeed, so we did everything we could to help; whether our actions were reasonable seemed to have nothing at all to do with it.

I could see by the set of his shoulders that he was very depressed.

'We've come to help you, Mr Paterson,' said Minnie.

'Go away, all of you,' he retorted.

'Things aren't so bad,' Ros said encouragingly.

'You were splendid in court,' I added, but this he ignored.

'I should never have come here. This is not the place. I've offended somehow. I must seek another path.'

'What are you going to do?' I asked, alarmed at the determination in his voice.

'I shall wait for the sign, and if there is none I shall move on, as I've done before, and shall do again. But I was so sure this was the place.' He spoke in a sad, wistful voice.

From the corner of my eye I saw Minnie tiptoe away towards the cottage. She slipped on a piece of shingle and almost fell, but Mr Paterson was so absorbed in his gloomy thoughts that he seemed conscious of nothing. I looked at Ros and she shook her head. I could see that she was not hopeful that anything could be done. But at that moment Minnie came out holding the shell, a huge and magnificent Triton, much more splendid than the illustration. She was smiling confidently, so I thought we might as well leave her to explain things, particularly as she believed you had only to imagine something for it to come true.

Mr Paterson continued to stare seawards, even when Minnie stood right beside him holding out the shell.

'What have you there?' he asked, so suddenly that Minnie nearly dropped it. 'Take care, Miranda; my father did not bring that shell all the way from the South Seas to have you hurl it carelessly to the ground.'

'It's no ordinary shell,' she said mysteriously.

'Then I would be obliged if you would kindly tell me what, in your opinion, it is.'

This was the opening Minnie was hoping for. She knelt down and stared rapturously into Mr Paterson's sombre face. 'This,' she cried dramatically, holding out the shell, 'is Neptune's horn.'

Although Mr Paterson did not move, I saw a flicker in his eyes. 'Explain yourself, Miranda.'

Minnie needed no encouragement and rattled on enthusiastically in a rather confused account of fish-calling and what the Romans believed about Neptune. The general drift was perfectly clear.

'If the fish come, that will show you the sea is listening. You can trust me because the gods have sent me as their messenger to show you the way.'

A fleeting smile lit the prophet's face. 'Very well, Messenger, you may tell me what I should do next.'

An absurd sense of relief swept over me like a warm tide. I knew then that things were far from over. I glanced at Ros; she was smiling too.

'You must first see if you can blow the shell,' said

64

Minnie, and she handed over her precious burden delicately, as if it was as fragile as an egg. I had a fancy then that the sound of the sea was oddly loud, and a wave broke so near us that the water's edge racing through the trembling shingle touched the hem of Mr Paterson's outspread robe. He stood up, holding the Triton, and his eyes were alight with a new fervour. I looked again at Ros, and saw the excitement in her face.

But Mr Paterson's first attempts to blow the shell were not encouraging. Putting it to his mouth he huffed and puffed, but no sound came out at all.

'The fish won't hear that,' said Minnie unnecessarily. I frowned at her to silence her.

'Perhaps you've got your thumb over the hole,' Ros suggested suddenly.

'Indeed I have not, Rosalind,' Mr Paterson replied, and put the shell to his lips once more. He tried and tried, holding the Triton this way and that and my first elation was replaced by a deep anxiety.

'I don't think you're breathing the right way,' Ros ventured at last. 'When we were taught singing we were made to breathe more from the solar plexus, not from the throat.'

Mr Paterson gave a sigh of irritation. 'I am not trying to sing, Rosalind.'

'But the same principles apply. I'm sure of it,' insisted Ros.

'Go on, try Ros's way,' cried Minnie.

Reluctantly at first, Mr Paterson practised breathing from his solar plexus. His breaths didn't look very different to me, but Ros was most enthusiastic.

'That's right. Much better. Now let's try the shell.' Anyone would think she was a singing teacher, the way she carried on.

So for at least the hundredth time, with a rather weary

expression, Mr Paterson raised the Triton to his lips. He took a deep breath Ros's way, and then blew steadily into the delicate rose-leaf interior.

The sound that emerged from that convoluted form was like nothing I had ever heard before, a curious hollow note, deep and haunting, as if the shell itself had let out a breath. Mr Paterson's hands trembled with excitement, and for one moment I thought he might drop the shell. He tried again, stronger this time, producing a marvellous, wild, thrilling call. If the ocean had a voice, it would be like this. I was sure of it. Again and again he blew, while overhead the gulls shrieked and dived, unsettled by the sound. A wind off the sea drove the waves at us until we had to retreat almost to the cottage door. Of course the tide was coming in, so there was nothing very extraordinary about that.

'I think,' said Mr Paterson, carefully laying the shell behind the door, 'that this calls for a celebration. Please collect some sticks, Miranda. We'll have tea. I'm parched after all that blowing.'

I suppose you have to pay for everything in this life, but another cup of Mr Paterson's tea seemed a high price. Somehow we managed to swallow it down, though I caught Ros pouring most of hers into a crack in the floor. Well, some people will always cheat. Minnie kept on asking what Mr Paterson was going to do with his new skill, but he didn't give her a proper answer, and in the end there was nothing we could do except leave him alone with his thoughts.

'I must await the correct moment,' was all he would say to our repeated enquiries.

'Don't leave it too long,' I warned.

'You've got to be out of here in a fortnight,' said Ros.

'Indeed I have information to that effect,' replied Mr Paterson, looking both sad and angry. And more than that he refused to say. Feeling slightly deflated, we walked back home along the sands.

 10

After the case the evening papers were pretty dreadful, but much as we expected. *PROPHET BOUND OVER. EVICTION ORDER SERVED ON NORTHBURGH HOLY MAN.* Martin Parker had not been idle. There was a lengthy account of the court proceedings and a distant, blurred photograph of Mr Paterson holding his hands before his eyes to keep his soul intact. There was also a mention of him on the local radio news and Mum saw something on the regional television. Whether he welcomed it or not, the world was beginning to take notice of Mr Paterson. He was not on the rock that evening, but the weather was dry so I took advantage of that to photograph one or two beach scenes. Mum and Minnie had gone to the local cinema and Ros was with Miss Jessop, practising Mendelssohn for the concert. Miss Jessop seemed to be keeping a much closer eye on Ros's musical progress which, to our unspoken relief, made the house more peaceful, although the tension of her anxiety about the scholarship never left it. I thought Ros was very lucky to care about something so intensely and that in a way was what she had in common with Mr Paterson.

That evening my imaginative eye was not working well. There is a limit to the number of times you can photograph seaweed in artistic shapes or rocks or pretty small children. I needed a new angle, a new light to lead me down an unknown path, so I waded out ankle deep to sit on Mr Paterson's rock. I wasn't expecting anything to happen, but it was very peaceful. I watched for a long time as far away ships steamed across my line of vision. A sailing boat bobbed in the distance, white as a cabbage butterfly. And then, far off on the sea wind, I heard the marvellous haunting voice of the Triton. Evidently Mr Paterson had been practising to good effect, for the notes were long drawn out yet somehow questioning. Surely the sea must give him an answer soon, or Neptune rise from the waves to reclaim his own. I sat and waited, hoping the call of the shell would come again. But it didn't, and not surprisingly, for as I waded back through the shallows, still in my long-suffering gym shoes, I saw Mr Paterson coming towards me along the tide's edge. He was walking rather fast and eagerly, and he was carrying the shell in his arms.

He gave me a brief nod by way of greeting and did not stop, so I fell in behind him. I wanted to see where he was going and what he was planning to do. He made no objection, although he quickened his pace so that I almost had to run to keep up with him.

As I drew level I asked, 'Where are you going?' several times, but he gave no answer, and I realised that I expected none. He wasn't going to our home, nor to the town centre, for he ignored the turning off to the road. Instead, he continued striding along the sands that led in the end to Northburgh's small but busy harbour.

A sudden anxiety seized me. 'What are you going to do?'

There was no reply except an increase in speed. He was very fit for an elderly man.

We were very near the harbour now. I could see the masts of the fishing boats, and some pretty holiday craft bobbing in the evening swell. At the far end of the harbour wall, which reached out into the sea like a long finger, was a small lighthouse which at night flashed and twinkled like a land-locked star. At the foot of the steps that led up to the wall Mr Paterson paused and turned to look at me, murmuring something about deep water being best. Then he launched himself rapidly up the steep stone steps, watched by some small boys and one or two old men, idly baiting their lines and enjoying the balmy evening air.

At the top of the steps Mr Paterson stopped and looked all round, catching the attention of some fishermen mending their nets and would-be sailors messing about in boats. Then he strode purposefully along the high breakwater towards the distant lighthouse. I followed at a tactful distance, not wanting to attract attention to myself. This was rather too public a place, I thought, for what I suspected Mr Paterson had in mind. And my fears proved right. Reaching the end of the wall, under the shadow of the lighthouse, he stood upright and commanding, staring out over the evening waves. It was, I had to admit, the perfect setting. In the sinking sun the waves were running gold-tipped across our line of vision, the slanting rays gilding the sails of returning yachts. A line of black-backed gulls settled on the wall, and for once ceased their endless chatter to stare with hard black eyes.

Slowly, Mr Paterson raised the Triton to his lips and blew long and hard. He had learnt his lesson well. Whether his breath came from the solar plexus or not, the note he produced was stunningly effective. Clear and sustained, it made me shiver with a strange excitement, and as the sound died away, people – as if drawn by a magnet – ceased whatever they were doing and hurried to join the small crowd of watchers already gathered on the wall. I waved to them to come quietly and positioned myself facing them, my back to Mr Paterson. Again he blew the Triton and again a curious shiver ran through the watchers. In the distance I could see more people making their way towards us.

'What's he doing?' someone asked, and as I could give him no sensible reply, he pushed past me. 'Hey, Prophet, what are you doing? Calling up old Father Neptune?'

For answer Mr Paterson put his horn to his lips and blew a really tremendous blast. A long silence followed, broken only by the mewing of the gulls.

'There's no one at home,' said a cruel voice and there was an unsympathetic gale of laughter. Mr Paterson paid no attention to them. He blew and blew, and I turned to stare at the uncaring sea, willing something to happen. I prayed to the only God I knew about, that if there was anyone there they would answer him. But only the sea wind answered, gusting sharply around us. And with the freshening of the wind I saw to my relief that the watchers were losing interest and wandering away, making less than complimentary remarks about prophets' powers. Only an old salt lingered. He was a small, squat man with fine grey eyes and a red face – not unlike the man in the photograph I had seen at the exhibition. I was glad there were still some of his kind in existence after all.

'I tell you, friend, the sea will answer. But in its own good time,' he said mysteriously.

I felt a small stir of hope. But Mr Paterson was not to be cheered. He had given up blowing and was leaning against the sea wall, his head bowed.

'Come away,' I urged. 'This cold wind won't do you any good.' I waited for ages, expecting him to come with me, but he showed no signs of moving.

'I'll have to go,' I said, 'I promised to get the supper for the others. They'll be back soon.'

But Mr Paterson's head remained bowed. He seemed not to have heard what I said but to be intent only on the shell cradled in his arms. They told me later that he stayed there alone long after the lighthouse began to flash its cheerful beacon over the cruel waves.

70

'Poor old fellow,' said Mum, when I told them about it all. 'I wonder where it will end.'

I think deep down they were very disappointed, for Ros and Minnie said nothing at all.

That night I thought long and hard about everything. And as I listened to the waves breaking on the sands beneath my window I could come to no satisfactory conclusion about the power of the Triton. I got out of bed several times to look, but all seemed as usual. I felt a sadness for Mr Paterson and yet . . . What did I really know of the sea? Come to that, what did I know about anything? I must look deeper into things, as he did, I thought, glancing round my gallery of photographs. I must try to discover their souls. That was the thing with Mr Paterson: he always made you think.

I went back to bed and tried to sleep. Eventually I did, but the sound of the shell, hollow and infinitely mysterious, pursued me through my dreams.

I I

In the end I must have slept heavily, for I did not wake until I heard the sound of shouting and running feet. Minnie burst into my room.

'William,' she shouted, 'it worked!' She was tugging at the bedclothes in a frantic effort to get me out. I sat up, pushing back sleep.

'What on earth, Minnie . . .?' I began.

'Get up and come and see,' she cried in exasperation. 'Don't just lie there, stupid, or you'll miss everything.' And she dashed away before I could ask her any details. I heard her shouting excitedly at Ros and Mum. I glanced at my watch. It was only seven o'clock, but I nevertheless heaved myself up, pulled on jeans, pullover and gym-shoes and tore down the stairs. The back door was already wide open and I could see in the distance the small figure of my sister running towards the harbour. I shouted to Ros and Mum. They were not far behind me as I raced to catch up with Minnie. When I did I gasped, 'What is it, Min?' I was very out of breath.

'I came back to get you. I went down early to see . . .' She was managing to speak while running even faster than before. 'After you told me about Mr Paterson blowing the shell. I went to have a look.'

We were nearly at the harbour steps now. I could see that even at this hour the wall was crowded with people, all of whom appeared to be staring directly into the water beneath. There was something in their attitude that made me put on a last spurt so that, easily outdistancing Minnie, I dashed up the steps. I pushed my way to the front of the crowd and looked down. For an instant I had an impression of a wild whirlpool, a frantic, turbulent activity in the normally peaceful water. But it was a tur-bulence not of water, nor wind, but of dolphins. The harbour was alive with them, packed together in the deep water, swimming and jumping, streaking wildly across the surface as if possessed, wheeling, turning, leaping. The dark, gleaming, lithe bodies made a thousand turns, twists and dives, the arched backs glinting in the early morning sun. Their curious, bright eyes, as their heads broke the surface, were full of some hidden knowledge, and their wide mouths were smiling, a strange with-drawn smile. Magically together, never touching, an intricately manoeuvred tarantella of the sea was their dance. The water was boiling with sprats, after which the dolphins darted and leapt with frantic pleasure.

I watched, stunned and silent, scarcely noticing Minnie come up beside me. She had pushed her impatient way through the crowd, announcing in her clear voice, 'I must get to my brother. He knows all about this.' Amazingly, they parted to let her through.

'Isn't it marvellous, William? Isn't it beautiful? Mr Paterson will be so thrilled.'

I realised then with a shock that just for a moment I had forgotten all about our friend and his part in the strange events. A dolphin leapt high and wild, opening wide its smiling mouth.

'They're after the sprats. That's all,' I said. I shall never forget the look that Minnie gave me then. It was like the time I accidentally let out her beloved pet mouse Rupert. I felt as I did then, a betrayer, a murderer. But it was worse, for this time I had trodden on a dream.

'If you won't tell Mr Paterson, then I will,' she said fiercely, and before I could stop her she dodged under my arm, pushed her way along the wall and ran down the steps towards his cottage.

More and more people were coming to see the strange sight. Mum and Ros arrived, having walked rather more sedately.

'Did you see Minnie?' I asked them anxiously.

'She was running like a mad thing towards Mr Paterson's.'

'She's gone to get him.'

'She hasn't far to go.' And Ros laughed.

'Why?'

'He's already half way along the beach. We saw him as we came out of the house. He'll be here any minute.'

We stood there watching the fevered dance. Then, only a few feet away along the wall, I saw the old sailor I had spoken to the evening before. He nodded to me.

'So your friend succeeded after all,' he said when I had edged close enough to hear him.

'But you don't believe it surely?' I was desperate for

reassurance of my own doubts.

'Perhaps.'

'But . . . why?'

'I've been a sailor all my life, see, and you learn about things that way. That you'll never know all there is. You're not sure about anything, not when you're at sea. And anyway my old dad used to tell us about seeing dolphins here years ago.'

There was no time to pursue our conversation, because at that moment a ripple of renewed interest passed through the assembled crowd. Mr Paterson emerged, tall and pale. The crowd parted to let him through and he stood motionless at the wall's edge, looking down into the boiling waters of the harbour. He was not carrying the shell. In the distance, equally intent but with his eyes not on the dolphins but on the Prophet of Northburgh, was Martin Parker. As I watched, he began threading his way through the crowd, and behind him was his acolyte: a bespectacled youth with a camera.

I tried to warn Mr Paterson, but he seemed hypnotised by the leaping dolphins, a faint smile playing on his lips. Martin Parker came right up to him.

'I wonder, Mr Paterson, if you would care to comment on what you see,' he said. Smoothly, the photographer sidled up behind, adjusting his lens.

'Comment?' echoed Mr Paterson. He turned to the reporter. There was a cold look in his eyes, but Martin Parker was not to be put off.

'This would seem to prove that fish-calling as an ancient art can still be practised with some success. Would you care to comment on that?'

'I would not,' snapped our prophet.

'But you were seen last night calling to the fish with your shell, and you can't deny —' He indicated the dolphins – 'that you appear to have succeeded. Where's it all

74

going to end? That's what we want to know.'

The photographer by this time had raised his camera. The lens glittered as the seeing eye pointed at its quarry.

'Look over here please, Mr Paterson,' called the youth.

'No! Wait! You mustn't,' I began. 'He hates —'

But I was too late. Mr Paterson swung round, saw what was about to happen and, with a shout of rage, leapt at the photographer, knocking the camera out of his hand and into the deep water of the harbour.

'Hey! That's valuable equipment. You've no right. It'll be ruined!' Martin Parker was shouting furiously at Mr Paterson while the photographer just stood looking dismayed and not a little foolish.

Mr Paterson ignored them both and, turning from the harbour's edge, he walked away through the crowd, which parted nervously to let him pass.

'He hates having his photograph taken. I tried to tell you,' I said.

Martin Parker looked angrily at me. 'You left it a bit late then, didn't you?'

I said I was sorry, but pointed out that the photographer really had only himself to blame and that it was nothing to do with Mr Paterson.

'It seems to me you know a lot more about that friend of yours than you're telling,' Martin Parker said nastily.

'Can't you leave him alone?' I appealed to the man who had come so humbly to our house that first day. 'We only told you about him because we thought you'd do him no harm.'

'He's the one that does harm.' There was a hard edge to his voice. 'Appealing to the superstitious element. I wouldn't be at all surprised if he doesn't get quite a following after this.' We watched Mr Paterson disappear down the steps. 'Look at that now.' Martin Parker sounded bitter. 'Not a soul tries to stop him. He ruins my equipment and they're all on his side. There's no justice, I tell you, no justice at all.'

At that moment there was a gasp from the crowd. I turned round in time to see the dolphins leaving. In one apparently orchestrated movement they wheeled and headed for the harbour mouth, a merry throng leaping joyfully for the open sea, the water drops glittering on their smooth backs. Far out, there was a patch of water caught in the rays of the sun, looking like an enchanted sea of Mr Paterson's memory. The dolphins swam away towards it without a backward glance, but if they could, I am sure they would have been laughing.

Everything about that morning's episode was very worrying, and we discussed it over lunch. Mum pointed out the obvious.

'What if they arrest Mr Paterson on an assault charge?' she said anxiously. 'He was bound over to keep the peace after all.'

'And he didn't,' agreed Minnie.

'But it wasn't his fault,' I protested. 'The photographer asked for it, coming up suddenly behind him like that.'

'Mrs Brewster won't like it,' said Ros gloomily.

'Perhaps I shouldn't have told him about the shell.' Minnie was thoroughly alarmed by our talk, and tears glistened in her eyes.

'You weren't to know, darling,' said Mum gently.

'And it could have been a coincidence,' I said, but I didn't sound very convincing.

'You don't really believe that, do you?' Ros always knows what I'm thinking.

I shrugged. 'I don't know what to believe any more.'

But the afternoon's news was even worse, for it seemed that the dolphins had gone on their merry way past the nets of the inshore fishermen and in one glorious spree had destroyed both nets and most of the catch. There were long faces all round the town, and Martin Parker had produced a biased and inaccurate account of Mr Paterson's behaviour for the evening paper. I bought it on my way back from the shops. *A PROPHET WHO DOES NOT CARE*, it said. I suppose he had his photographer to think of, but I had expected better of Martin Parker. At home I found Mum had made a pie for Mr Paterson.

'With all this worry he won't have had time to eat,' she explained. I took the pie gratefully. My mother was really very good sometimes.

Mr Paterson was sitting on the shingle outside his cottage, the shell tucked into the folds of his robe. I showed him the pie. He told me to put it in front of the fire.

'I must try again,' he said.

'Do you – do you think you ought to? I mean, they say the nets were destroyed by the dolphins. Think what might happen if you called them again. The fishermen might turn really nasty.'

'But I've so little time left to practise,' he said unexpectedly.

'Practise?' I repeated after him, stupidly. 'What for?' A doubt stirred in my mind. What was he planning now? He seemed to read my thoughts.

'You surely can't think, William, that calling a few dolphins is the end of all this.'

I was completely taken aback. 'Then what is?'

For a moment he didn't answer, but touched the rough, grained surface of the shell. 'Soon I'll show you, show all of you. Then the world will have proof of my beliefs.'

'Proof?' Something in his voice made my heart beat fast. 'Please, Mr Paterson, tell me what you mean.'

He was on his feet, his head flung back with a strange exultation. 'What do I care for summonses and petty jealousies! I know now that I have been sent to open the eyes of the unbeliever. It is my destiny. The gods have spoken.'

He sounded so wild that I backed away out of reach. I didn't dare ask him to explain any more, but I felt I must try to persuade him to stop doing whatever he was going to do by reminding him of the consequences of his latest action. 'They'll probably insist that you pay for the camera. They may even –' I stopped. He was staring at me as if he scarcely knew who I was. 'Don't forget to eat the pie,' I told him.

For answer he put the shell to his lips and began to blow like a man possessed.

The dolphins did not come again, or anything else. But Mr Paterson's fragile peace was in ruins. Now there were watchers with binoculars on the shore and crowds outside his door begging him to blow his magic shell. As the days passed we watched him grow perceptibly thinner and older. He seemed strangely weary, too, and it was not long before he gave up altogether and sat motionless, the shell cradled in his arms. Minnie went to visit him every morning, but he was as silent and remote as the rocks, staring endlessly out to sea and never once speaking or raising the shell to his lips. Often when she returned, her face was red and swollen from crying.

The only good thing about those troubled days was the weather. Ever since the coming of the dolphins the sun had shone ceaselessly and the summer visitors basked in ever increasing numbers on the pale sands. The beach was noisy with the cries and shouts of bathers, the barking of excited dogs and children shrieking as their paper kites soared and swooped in the balmy winds. I bought a

78

pair of sun-glasses in the local chemists. They were expensive, but I thought they suited me.

'You think you look so grown-up and soph —' Minnie concealed the fact that she couldn't pronounce the word in her scornful tone.

'Oh shut up,' I snapped. 'You're just jealous.' I had had enough of Minnie lately, and Ros's renewed practising was getting on all our nerves.

'Children, children,' reproved Mum. 'It's too hot to quarrel.'

I didn't like being called a child, but she was right.

'Come on, cheer up,' she added. 'Nothing lasts for ever. Something's bound to happen soon.' And she spoke more truthfully than she knew, because the very next day something did.

A Mr Antony Beaton of Mercia Television came to our door and knocked.

 12

Mr Antony Beaton was the politest man I had ever met. He knocked in such a diffident way, as if he did not really want to come in and would rather not attempt the door bell. I opened the door to see a slight man in a suede jacket. He had a mop of curly dark hair and tinted spectacles.

'Antony Beaton, Mercia Television,' he said in a light, pleasant voice, proffering his hand.

'Who is it?' called Mum.

'It's someone from the television.'

'So sorry to disturb you,' the visitor said apologetically, adding, 'You are William Seaward? May I call you William?'

I thought it was a little early for Christian names, but I

79

said yes. There wasn't much else I could have said. And Antony Beaton wasn't like Martin Parker, all push and thrust. He hovered shyly on the threshold until invited in. We were in the kitchen as usual. Once inside he advanced nervously to shake Mum's hand, then Ros's, then Minnie's. I could see that Mum liked him right away, by the way she was smiling. She put on some more coffee and he sat down where she told him. He went on and on about what a lovely family we were, so talented, how marvellous to play the violin, photography being such a fascinating subject. He seemed to know a great deal about us.

'And what are you good at, Miranda?' He turned his intent gaze on Minnie. It was rather a difficult question, but of course she was quite equal to the situation.

'I'm very good at making friends and I am a Messenger of the Gods.'

'Minnie, what are you saying?' gasped Mum, but Minnie only smiled and put on her sprite's face, which was very winning.

Antony Beaton leant forward, tense with an interest that was genuine. 'Tell me, what do you mean by that, Miranda? I long to know, I absolutely long.'

And before we knew it Minnie had told him all about Mr Paterson and his adventures. She hadn't learnt a thing from our experiences with Martin Parker. Yet it was not altogether bad. Better for Mr Beaton to hear about it from Minnie's admiring and uncritical viewpoint than from Mrs Brewster or, worse still, Martin Parker. We let her continue. We couldn't have stopped her anyway.

'Most enthralling, I must say,' said Antony Beaton, when she had finished her long excited tale. 'And you tell it so extremely well, if I may say so. We'll have you on our magic box one of these days. You'd be a natural.'

80

I caught Ros's eye and I knew that we were both thinking Minnie would be even more impossible after this.

Mr Beaton then turned his attention to me. 'This house of shells that your sister described. Do you think your Mr Paterson would let us see inside?'

'Why do you want to?' I was beginning to be very suspicious.

'A good question, William. And I will explain. You see, we are doing a series of programmes on interesting, even exceptional, people called 'A Different View' – a good title, you will agree.' He didn't wait for an answer. 'I think your Mr Paterson would be an excellent subject. He has a great deal to contribute, and in the circumstances it might even prove a help. The authorities are hardly likely to turn him out while our cameras are there, are they?'

'Oh, you've heard about that?' Mum sounded surprised. Antony Beaton flushed and went on hastily.

'I spoke to a Mrs Brewster, and I have to say that it was not a success. She seemed to think I would want her on the programme as the town's most celebrated citizen.'

'You can't.' Ros was horrified.

'Have no fear, Rosalind. No such disaster will befall. Mrs Brewster's mind runs on steel rails – fast, mark you, but dead straight. No corners, not a siding in sight. Absolutely terrifying. If you lay down on the line she wouldn't stop.' He gave a nervous laugh. 'Actually I thought Mr Brewster by far the more interesting of the two, but there are some fences that even I will not jump.'

Mum was replenishing the coffee and had her back to us. She turned and looked directly at Mr Beaton. 'Then why have you come to us? Surely it's Mr Paterson you should see.'

There was a long silence and Antony Beaton fiddled with his spectacles. He looked embarrassed. 'I have, dear lady, but he was – that is, he didn't want to know. Actually he was rather offensive. He told me where to go and a great many other rather more personal things.'

'So you want us to persuade him for you? That's it, isn't it?' I said.

'In a nutshell, yes.'

Mum brought the coffee to the table, her face troubled. 'I don't know if you can ask my children to do that. They are his friends. I am, too, for that matter, and we can't betray a friend.'

For a moment Antony Beaton looked put out. Then he tipped back his chair and said, 'No one is asking you to betray a friend. I only want you to have a go at persuading him, and if it fails, well —' He gave a slight shrug — 'fortunes of war, everyone, fortunes of war.' He managed to look both pathetic and heroic at the same time.

'I suppose we might . . .' began Ros, who was always kind.

'But only if it would help him,' I said uncertainly.

'Of course it would help,' cried our visitor enthusiastically. 'He's got no money, has he, and we are not exactly poor, you understand. And if your friend wants to publicise his message, what better way? For that kind of thing media exposure is an essential element these days.'

This was undeniably true, yet at the back of my mind I kept thinking about Mr Paterson's determination to produce his proof. A tiny seed of doubt grew, although it seemed logical and even helpful to agree to Antony Beaton's request.

'There is one thing though,' said Ros.

'And what is that?' He looked at Ros with frankly admiring eyes.

'He hates being photographed.' Mr Beaton's face fell, but only for an instant.

'Oh dear. That's certainly a problem, but we'll overcome, I dare say. All you artistic people are the same. One must just know how to handle things, that's all.' He smiled at Ros. 'And I shall make a point of hearing you play at the concert.'

'No, don't, please.' Ros frowned, but Mr Beaton was already on his feet, holding out his hand, suddenly brisk and efficient.

'That's fixed then. You'll have a word with your friend as soon as you can and I'll telephone tomorrow to see how you got on. Goodbye, everyone.'

And he was gone. We watched him drive away in a new green BMW.

'Goodbye,' said Mum, gazing after him with an expression on her face that I could not read.

Now we had only one thing to decide and that was who was going to ask Mr Paterson about appearing on television.

'Ros has too much on her mind, so it will have to be you, William,' said Mum firmly. The concert was only a day away.

'What about me?' Minnie was indignant, but in this at least she was not going to get her way. I was to go, and, there being no time like the present for a difficult task, I set off at once. But there was no sign of Mr Paterson at the fisherman's cottage. The place was deserted. A sudden fear gripped me. Had he gone already? I couldn't really have blamed him if he had. Then I heard a voice calling faintly from the direction of the sea, almost under the cliffs. To my dismay I saw Mr Paterson sitting hunched in a rowing boat, vainly trying to manipulate the oars to push himself afloat. I raced to the sea's edge.

'Please, William, help me to get to sea.'

'In that old sieve?' I said, looking at the ancient boat buckled with time and sea water and already leaking.

'My craft will suffice. I borrowed it from a fisherman and he said it was sound enough.'

'You can't go out alone in that thing,' I said. 'You'll never manage.'

The deep-set eyes were turned to me. 'Then you'll come with me?'

I suppose I should have refused then and there, but there was something in his expression that interested me.

'Not at this moment. I've got things to do,' I said evasively.

'Later, perhaps,' he said, cunningly adding, 'You can tell me what you have come to say and I will give you my answer when you return to go out in the boat.'

'How did you know I've got something to say?' I asked. 'And why do you want to put to sea?'

But he only smiled and shipped the oars.

So I explained about Mr Beaton and his programme and went through all the advantages and disadvantages. He heard me out in silence.

Then he said, 'A prophet must tread his path alone.'

'You could do with the money.'

'I have sufficient for my needs.'

'Not if there is all that photographic equipment to replace.' I thought that was a stroke of genius on my part.

'You are a dear friend, William,' he said gently, managing to look forlorn and vulnerable as the rickety boat in which he sat.

I sighed. 'What is it you want me to do?'

His eyes were alight with enthusiasm, the bony hands gripping the edge of the boat as he told me how he wanted to go out to the deep water where no one could see or hear, and call again with the shell in a new way he had discovered.

'It won't be easy,' I said uncertainly.

'With you at the oars, anything is possible,' he replied,

stepping gingerly from the beached boat. 'Until later then.' And he walked away without looking back.

How, I asked myself all the way home, did I get myself into these situations. I decided to say as little as possible to the others, except to tell Ros that I had delivered my message and was due to return for an answer later.

We spent a pleasant evening, just as we used to before Mr Paterson came into our lives. Mum was laughing and carefree and Ros was more relaxed than she had been for ages. And Minnie surprised us all by making the supper. Not very well, mind you, but not bad for one so young.

Yet throughout it all I found myself thinking about Dad and how he would have known what to do. Oh, why did everything have to change? Why did nothing ever stay the same?

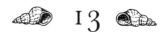 13

I waited until Minnie was asleep and Mum absorbed in her favourite television programme before I left the house. I hurried along the deserted sands, for it was well after ten o'clock. There is something special about a summer night by the sea. The moon shone a silver pathway down the water and phosphorescence tipped the running ripples. True to his word, Mr Paterson was waiting for me by the boat. He was holding the shell, so I told him to get in, then pushed us out into deeper water before I got in and took up the oars. I had taken the precaution of bringing the kettle to bale us out should the need arise.

'Where do you want to go?'

'As far as you feel you can row.'

It was easy with the ebbing tide. There was a marvellous listening silence about us, and the splashing of the oars and the far away sound of waves breaking under the cliff. Mr Paterson sat quiet and remote, his face raised to the night sky. Soon we had gone quite a fair distance and I could see the lights of Northburgh along the shore to my right.

'Will this do?' I asked, but I was already shipping the oars. We had gone far enough, what with the leaking boat and Mr Paterson being unable to swim.

For answer he abruptly stood upright. 'Careful,' I cried, 'or you'll have us both in.'

But he didn't seem to hear and, raising the Triton to his lips, he blew some short rhythmic notes, then a long soul seeker of a sound, deep and thrilling.

Time passed and I took no account of it. Now there was only the night and the sea and the voice of the shell. The boat leaked a little and I had to reach for the baler. The notes of the shell died away and my passenger stared into the blackness of the open sea. There was a waiting feel to the air. Then in the distance, just above the silvery waves, I saw a long dark shape heading straight at us. Something had heard the call of the shell and it was very large indeed. Sweat beaded my forehead and my hands trembled. Mr Paterson was staring transfixed, as if unable to believe what was happening. The leaky boat dipped and rolled in the swell. I let go of the baler and seized the oars. Suddenly the night seemed full of sounds: the splash of the water, the scrape of wood in the battered rowlocks. I glanced over my shoulder; the dark shape was nearer and the shore was a hundred miles away. I began to row with all the strength that I possessed. If I did not reach land we would both be drowned here in the dark.

The moon shone clear as the huge fish passed close to the boat and I could just make out the mottle markings of a basking shark. The well of its passing nearly sank us, but Mr Paterson stood up again, waving the shell in a

86

crazy kind of triumph.

'For God's sake!' I shouted as, unbelievably, he put it to his lips and blew again. The great fish turned with a slap of its tail and headed straight back for us. It was a nightmare from which is no wakening. In another second the boat would be over.

Then Mr Paterson did something so splendid and tragic that I marvel at it yet. Just as the creature reached us and I looked into its cold and shining eye, he flung the precious shell straight at the wide head. The shark sank immediately as if depth-charged and stole away as silently and mysteriously as it had come. We were safe, but in the shifting ocean bed the Triton shell lay lost to us for ever.

'*Full fathom five thy father lies,*' said Mr Paterson in a broken voice. He had sunk down on his knees in the bottom of the boat and was staring into the dark depths of the water that held his treasure. The sea round us subsided. I was uncomfortably aware that the pool of water inside our craft was very much bigger. If we did not get ashore soon we would join the shell.

I began to row frantically and I was glad of that because it left me no breath to speak. I was almost at the end of my strength, for the boat was leaden with the weight of so much water. When we scraped along the slope of the beach it was the sweetest sound I ever heard. All the time Mr Paterson sat unmoving and silent in the bows. He didn't speak when I helped him unsteadily on to the beach. I could feel the frightening thinness of his arm and felt a surge of pity. I wondered what this new misfortune would do to him.

I stood, uncertain what to do next. He still seemed dazed and the trailing robe was sodden with sea water. So I helped him gently into the cottage and while he sat hunched upon the sandy floor searched around for wood and dried seaweed for a fire. I found an old broken plank studded with ancient copper nails. When I had piled sufficient into the grate I put a match to it. The dried weed flared and sparked and ignited the salt-impregnated wood, and the copper nails gave off a strange bluish flame which flickered and danced on the glimmering shell walls. The mother of pearl caught the light for all the world as if we two were at the bottom of the sea. Outside it was ominously hushed and quiet, the distant throb of the breakers on the shore was like the beating of a heart.

I fetched in the kettle, but it had sprung a leak and was no more use. I wished that Mr Paterson would say something, anything, to break the uneasy silence that held us both. I poked at the fire and the fierce blue flame cruelly illuminated the gaunt hollows of his face and the despair in the blank eyes.

Then he murmured something so softly that I could scarcely catch the words. 'Man is born with a dream.'

'A dream?' I prompted.

'Which fills his mind, runs through his veins like sap and then . . .'

'And then?' The greenish eyes focused on me wearily.

'The years press, the dream fades and is altogether lost.' He fell silent, but I could not leave it there.

'You haven't lost your dream, Mr Paterson.'

He smiled, and for a moment looked almost young. Then he got stiffly to his feet and stood in the open door, leaning against the twisted lintel. His eyes were on the sea and his voice seemed to come from far off.

'I thought I had, William, until the first morning I was here. I remember that day. The sea was flat calm and on the surface hung a curtain of mist so light, so delicate, and so far away. But as I stood watching, a wind got up and the mist stole in towards me like a company of ghosts.

88

Their cold fingers were on my cheek, my eyes were full of their tears. Then the sun rose, the mist dissolved, but my dream was returned to me. Such a beautiful dream.' The voice died away, but I wouldn't let him stop.

'Please,' I said, 'what was your dream?'

'Of a world green as grass and water clear as a good man's soul. No sound but the voice of wind . . .'

The brightness of his vision faded. His voice was full of regret. 'I could have brought it all back with my shell. I had learnt how to call and the old world would have answered me.'

It was too painful for him to continue. A tear ran with terrible slowness down his lined cheek. He hunched by the dying fire like a bag of driftwood.

'We can get back the shell by diving for it.' My words came tumbling out, though even as I spoke I did not believe what I was saying. It was over. The dream was ended.

He seemed to read my thoughts. 'You can tell your television friend that I shall not be appearing on his programme.' Then he muttered something that sounded like *Eyes of the forest*. I didn't understand, but to my repeated questions there was no answer and in the end I left him to his sorrow.

It had started to rain and a cold wind blew off the sea so that by the time I reached home the night was roaring on the land and the rain was like a curtain. I was very glad to be ashore and home again. Mum was waiting for me, white-faced with anxiety.

'William, where have you been for so long? What have you been doing? You look half drowned.'

I was glad of the rain to explain the drops of water on my cheeks.

'You look exhausted, darling. Something dreadful has happened. I can tell by your face. I've just got it out of

89

Ros that you might be with Mr Paterson. I was coming to fetch you.' Her voice was shrill with tension. 'I didn't know what was best. I do know, though, that I don't want Ros worried. It's her concert tomorrow.'

In all the excitement I had completely forgotten about that. 'Let me get my things off, and then I'll tell you,' I said as calmly as I could.

'I'll make us some cocoa.' She still sounded very upset.

So over the cocoa I told Mum and Ros all that had happened. They listened in silence.

'Poor Mr Paterson. Nothing ever seems to go right for him. But it was so dangerous, William, to go out in that boat. I can't bear to think of it,' said Mum.

'He'll never do the programme now, so he won't get any money.'

'Perhaps it's just not meant.'

'And now he'll go.' I voiced my deepest fear.

'I expect he will,' said Mum slowly. Outside the wind struck the window like a blow.

'Just listen to that. The gods are really angry.' Ros spoke in an odd way and I saw she had an abstracted look. I didn't want to upset her any more, so I said, 'There's nothing any of us can do. The sea has reclaimed its own.'

'I wonder,' answered Ros reflectively, 'if you are right.'

'What do you mean, dear?' asked Mum, but Ros only shook her head and wouldn't explain.

I was very tired so I went to bed then. For a long time I lay awake listening to the storm, and I thought about what Ros had said but could make nothing of it. Still in my mind's pitiless eye I could see the boat and the shape of the shark and the splintered moon on the dark water. And through the crash of the waves and the scream of the wind I saw the Triton shell lying beneath the waters, the beautiful, mysterious voice silenced for ever, the rose-petal mouth choked with shifting sand.

The following morning the weather had not improved. The rain was coming down in sheets and the wind howled round the house, driving in huge grey seas and lashing the wave tops. I hated to think what it must be like at the fisherman's cottage. But today, at least, everything was for Ros. Nothing must be allowed to disturb her concentration. Mum had the day off and over breakfast we tried to be as normal as possible.

'A shame it's such a rotten day,' Minnie announced. She is not good at being tactful. 'No one will want to go out in this rain,' she continued, ignoring Mum's disapproving looks.

'Nonsense, dear. The place will be packed. There's nothing you can do outside on a day like this. At least the school will be dry and warm.'

'Thanks,' said Ros shortly.

'Oh, I didn't mean . . .' began Mum, then decided to say no more. There really wasn't any point, seeing Ros's pale, tense face and her hands clenching and unclenching. It must have been awful to have so much hanging on a single performance. Ros went upstairs immediately after breakfast and practised continually until lunch. I wasn't happy with what I heard. She kept repeating a single phrase until I thought we'd all go mad.

But eventually it was time for Ros to go. Miss Jessop was coming to collect her for a last rehearsal and then we were all to come later for the performance at seven o'clock.

'You've got the tickets, haven't you?' she asked. She held her violin under her arm and her dress for the performance was in her suitcase. She had washed her hair and it was still damp. I wondered if she had been crying, for her eyes were red-rimmed. But it might have been the soap. We had four tickets, an extra one for Mrs Woodstock who worked in the shop with Mum.

'We'll be there,' said Mum, as Miss Jessop blew her car horn and Ros dashed out, head down against the driving rain.

At tea time Mrs Woodstock rang to say she couldn't make the concert after all. She wasn't feeling too good.

'Shall we find someone else?' asked Mum.

'It's a bit late.'

'I think we should keep it just in case,' said Minnie.

'In case of what?' I asked, but she only shrugged.

We arrived at the hall in very good time. Mum had been right in her supposition that the poor weather would have a good effect on attendance. Besides proud parents in the audience there were many holiday visitors and a crowd of local people. The family of the soloist had seats near the front and if we hadn't been so anxious we would have enjoyed our reflected glory. The fourth unused seat was next to the gangway. Minnie had insisted on this for some mysterious reason of her own.

We settled down to watch the crowd assemble, as the wind continued to shake and rattle the windows in angry gusts. The very front row remained empty for eminent visitors, the head of the school and the festival director. Martin Parker was wandering about looking official. He avoided my eye. Then Antony Beaton arrived and acknowledged our presence with a careless wave of the hand, but did not come over to speak. He, too, sat near the front. I wondered what he was thinking, for I had taken the easy way out and left a message at Mercia House that Mr Paterson would not appear in his programme. Minnie complained loudly about there being no ice-creams or fizzy drinks.

'This is a concert, not a cinema,' said Mum firmly, but

92

she did have sweets in her pocket which she handed out to both of us.

There was a sudden stir of interest and, glancing round, I saw that the distinguished visitors had arrived, accompanied by Mrs Brewster, resplendent in black velvet dress and pearls. There were various important-looking people who most probably came from the music world. But as they took their seats there was a noisy commotion at the door, the sound of raised voices and cries of 'You can't come in without a ticket.' We turned round to see Mr Paterson advancing purposefully down the aisle, shaking off restraining hands and ignoring angry commands to leave the hall. He was wearing Father's cloak, and the shell band round his matted hair. I stood up, pointing to the empty seat beside us and he sank into it gratefully. I shall never forget Mrs Brewster's face, and Antony Beaton was like a man who cannot believe his own good fortune. Minnie was next to Mr Paterson and I saw her pat his hand in a friendly, welcoming way as if she had been expecting him.

Now the orchestra was filing on to the platform for the overture and Miss Jessop was calling us to silence. She gave a warm welcome to the visitors, who acknowledged her words with a gracious nod. She then explained to her audience that this was to be an evening with Mendelssohn. She made it sound as if he was actually here. I saw Mum smile, and Miss Jessop went on.

'We are going to begin with *Fingal's Cave*, the *Hebridean Overture*, and I must say it sounds as though the elements are responding.' We laughed politely at her little joke, the lights dimmed and the concert began in earnest.

I don't know how familiar the school orchestra was with the intricacies of Mendelssohn, for there were several uneven passages, but they set about it with a gusto which drowned out the wind and rain. I don't think

Mendelssohn would have been too disheartened. At least they all finished together. Antony Beaton looked rather bored and kept glancing at his watch, and Mrs Brewster stared straight ahead, giving nothing away. The orchestra trooped out for a brief rest before the Mendelssohn Violin Concerto for which Ros was playing the solo part.

'I feel sick,' announced Minnie loudly. 'And it's not too many sweets. I feel sick for Ros.'

We all did, and I wished I was somewhere else. The orchestra returned and tuned up, Miss Jessop mounted the rostrum and nodded to the wings and Ros came on. The audience gave a kind of gasp, for I had never seen her look so beautiful. Her hair glinted in the bright lights. She wore a long white dress of some filmy material. Her face was dreadfully pale, but her large eyes shone. She seemed almost unreal, like a spirit from another world. I saw Antony Beaton lean forward. He didn't look at all bored now. Miss Jessop tapped on the rostrum and Ros raised her violin, tucking it under her chin.

The audience grew quiet. With a firm downbeat Miss Jessop launched the orchestra and soloist into the Violin Concerto, which is one of those concertos where the solo instrument comes in straight away, no messing about. No chance to sort out your thoughts while the opening music flies about your head. Ros opened her eyes wide and began. She played well and accurately, but it was as if her feeling for the music stopped short at the bow. I could see that her arm was tense and her face sombre as if the music were somehow a duty to be performed. It was obvious that was how the audience began to feel, too, and one distinguished visitor shook his head, studying his fingernails. I could not look at Minnie or Mum. Outside, the wind shrieked without ceasing.

Then, without warning, Mr Paterson stood up, staring straight at Ros, holding out his arms in a kind of strange supplication. Her eyes flickered in acknowledgement. Her arm paused briefly, she glanced at the dark window and I thought she was going to lose a note. The orchestra faltered. Miss Jessop's beat was imperious, with a determination I could hardly bear to watch. Mum shut her eyes in pain. Mr Paterson subsided. Then, as if by some strange magic, not notes but real music began to pour from Ros's violin, a haunting disturbing voice to twist our very souls. We could all feel it, and as my sister played I realised by the faint smile on her lips that she knew she held us in the hollow of her hand. Like the night on the hill when Mr Paterson told her to play what she felt. She had stood then at the door to an enchanted land, but tonight, at this very moment, she had crossed a threshold where few ever go. She would never really return to us again. The slow movement came to a delicate, sighing close, followed by a difficult cadenza before Ros launched into the brilliant final movement. The glittering notes fell like stars from a Roman candle; we were caught in the golden net she wove – surely even the gods must have understood. I looked at Mum, who had tears in her eyes. Mr Paterson sat with his arms folded on his chest, looking like a man for whom the world has nothing better to offer. Too soon it was all over. Ros played the last notes softly, stroking them to a close, until they were no more than echoes in the mind.

The applause was deafening. We may not all have been musicians, but we knew instinctively that something marvellous had happened. We clapped and clapped, and Ros stared at us in a dazed kind of way as if she had just returned from that far away place and couldn't quite remember where she was. She looked across at Mr Paterson and I saw a glance of pure understanding pass between them like a flash of light. The applause was unceasing. Antony Beaton was on his feet. Ros bowed and bowed, her long hair falling over her face. Miss Jessop summoned the orchestra to rise and they, too, were smiling in the knowledge that this had been a very special event.

At last the applause died away and there was silence as the headmaster rose to make a speech of thanks. He was a pleasing man with an elegant manner, and he did not forget to thank the organisers and the stewards of the hall. He congratulated the orchestra and then turned to Ros. He didn't say anything in a fulsome way, just that he had no doubt he would be hearing more of her. 'Why,' he said, gesturing to the windows, 'she has even stilled the elements with her playing.'

And he was right. The wind had dropped; there was no more rain in the summer dusk. I glanced at Mr Paterson. Now that the music was over he looked old and defeated and clutched the cloak around him as if he were cold, even in that stifling hall.

After the concert there were refreshments, at the back of the hall. We felt rather proud as so many people came to congratulate us on Ros's performance. Mr Paterson was a bit of an embarrassment, not answering any pleasantries and eating the sandwiches rather fast, and more than his fair share, but I suppose it was ages since he had had anything to eat. Mrs Brewster kept her distance. Antony Beaton was standing with a small knot of people, talking hard, though I had the impression that he was watching us very closely. Ros came in. She had not changed out of her white dress. Beads of sweat still shone on her forehead and her hair was damp. She told us how nice the audience had been and how delighted Miss Jessop was, but she had an odd excited look in her eyes that did not come entirely from her reception and the fact that the ordeal was over.

'What happened to you?' I asked. 'What made you play like that?'

I was going to ask more, but people were advancing on us and Mum said it was nearly time to go. Besides, Mr Paterson looked tired, out of place and uncomfortable because of all the curious stares. So we said our goodbyes to Miss Jessop and the headmaster and went outside. Ros seemed impatient to be gone.

'You'll catch cold in that dress,' Mum told her.

'Of course I won't.'

'I think you magicked the weather,' said Minnie. 'It was awful when we came.'

Ros smiled, but the evening had indeed turned out perfectly: warm and balmy, and the evening star shone out over a flat, calm sea. Mr Paterson walked with us, but when we reached our house he declined an invitation to come in.

'It is kind of you,' he said, 'but I have to make preparations for my departure.'

Although I had in a way been expecting it, the words came as an almost physical blow. 'You can't go, not tonight.'

'I must be away before suffering the indignity of being turned out,' he said.

'But you can't go, you can't leave us. You mustn't.' Minnie was near to tears.

'Spend tonight with us, please,' begged Mum. 'We'll see what tomorrow brings.'

'Tomorrow will be too late.'

'Where will you go? Where will you stay?' But he had no answer to these questions.

'Do come in for a little while, or at least let us come with you to the cottage,' Mum suggested, and we walked slowly towards the sands.

'But if you go, what about your shells?' asked Minnie in a sad voice. Mr Paterson looked depressed.

'That may prove rather a difficulty. The properties of Superglue are undeniable.'

By now Ros was well ahead of us, running, her white dress gleaming in the summer night. She didn't seem at all tired.

'She played well, didn't she,' said Mum.

'Those whom the gods love,' said Mr Paterson mysteriously, and he imperceptibly quickened his pace as if he would catch up with Ros.

We walked then in silence, rather slowly, as if we did not wish the journey to end. Ros was first over the rocks that led to the cottage. I couldn't understand why she was in such a hurry. She was still clutching her precious violin.

'She'll fall if she doesn't watch out,' warned Minnie, as she disappeared from sight. We were all totally unprepared for Ros's wild cry, that echoed on the night air.

'She has fallen!' cried Mum.

But Mr Paterson tensed with a sudden excitement before leaping away from us over the rocks.

'Wait for me!' cried Mum, but she had to manage for herself. Minnie and I reached the shingle beach at the same time and I saw what had made Ros cry out. On the pebbles at her feet lay the Triton shell. Unharmed. For an instant Mr Paterson stood stone still. Then he knelt on the wet stones, hugging the shell to him like a drowned child.

'What the sea has taken, it has given back.' And there were tears in his cracked voice. He looked straight at Ros. 'I knew they could not possibly resist you.'

'I thought I wasn't going to manage until you came,' she said.

I wondered what he meant, but there was no time to

ask, for Ros took out her violin and began to play. The voice of the violin sang in my head, just as it had that night on the hill. At last I understood. The gods, if gods there were, had answered her prayer in their own inscrutable way.

Merrily, merrily shall I live now, under the blossom that hangs on the bough. Again, the golden net ensnared us all.

'A scene from enchantment's isle.' An unfamiliar voice broke the spell and Antony Beaton appeared without warning over the rocks. 'So this is where you all are. Really it's too much, too much. A prophet of the old world, the nymph with the violin, the mother, the photographer . . .' He paused, leaning forward.

'And a Messenger of the Gods,' cried Minnie, not to be left out.

Mr Beaton advanced towards us with a triumphant smile. 'You shan't escape me this time. I see the shell is miraculously returned. Now you surely owe it to the world to tell us your beliefs.'

'But I have to leave. They're going to throw me out,' said Mr Paterson.

'I'll fix that. Don't you fret. There'll be no eviction while I'm around; bad publicity. Besides, that reporter sees things my way now.' And he gave a broad wink.

'I don't know,' began Mr Paterson doubtfully, but Antony Beaton did not wait for an answer. He pushed past us, into the house of shells, shining his torch round the walls, his cries of 'Fantastic', 'Astonishing' echoing on the still air.

'You'd better give up, Mr Paterson. You're no match for such an enthusiast.' Mum smiled, as Mr Beaton stood dramatically in the doorway.

But Mr Paterson still hesitated, both hands cradling the shell. Then, without looking at any of us, he nodded. 'I'll do your programme. If you'll all kindly go now and leave me to my thoughts.' He sounded exhausted.

'But your soul,' I said. 'The camera will steal your soul.'

He looked at me then, and I saw the realisation in his eyes. But even as I spoke I remembered the new glasses I kept in my pocket, hopeful of the sun's return. I held them out, and after a moment's pause he took them from me.

'As through a glass darkly; I thank you, William,' he said.

On our way back Antony Beaton said in a wearied voice, 'I hope he won't wear those glasses for my film.'

'I think he will.'

'But he has such interesting eyes, it would be a tremendous pity to hide them.'

'He's afraid for his soul,' I replied. There was no other way of explaining.

Mr Beaton sighed. 'I should have known that this was not going to be my easiest assignment.'

Mum and Minnie went straight to bed when we got home, but Ros and I sat talking, for she was still much too excited to sleep.

'What happened to you tonight, Ros?'

'You mean, when Mr Paterson stood up?' For a moment I thought she wasn't going to answer me. Then she said, 'You mustn't laugh.'

'Of course I won't laugh.'

She didn't speak for ages, before continuing, 'It's not easy to explain. At the beginning I couldn't seem to hear what I was playing. And the bow felt so heavy – that's nothing new, it does happen to people when the music is not getting through to them.' She frowned at the memory. 'I knew I had to do something. I could feel someone or something calling me and I couldn't understand what it was or what they wanted.'

100

'Wanted? What on earth do you mean?'

Still she didn't elaborate. 'It sounds so unbelievable,' she whispered.

'Please, Ros,' I begged.

'Well, when Mr Paterson stood up, holding out his hands, I saw the shell very clearly, lying at the bottom of the sea on a patch of sand beside a rock. I remembered that night on the hill when Mr Paterson told me to play what I felt. So I did. I played for the lost shell and how we must ask the sea to give it back. And by the end I knew I'd done it. I don't know how, I just knew. The wind had stopped and I could see the shell lying there on the shingle.'

'But you can't have,' I interrupted. 'You were in the hall.'

'I told you it was ridiculous, but I did see it. I did.'

I tried to speak, but no words came.

'Something brought back the shell,' said Ros. 'And if it wasn't my playing, what was it?'

She was pushing back her hair with her hand. She looked very white and tired now. But suddenly almost grown up. I had no answer. I felt then, for the first time, that her music was a barrier between us.

Long after she had gone upstairs I sat thinking, trying in vain to fathom the answer to Ros's question. She had said she understood, as she played, that we must ask the sea to give back the shell, and it had. But that didn't make sense. At least, not to me. But Ros believed it, and Mr Paterson believed it. Was that why he had finally consented to appear on the programme? Perhaps Antony Beaton was right, and now that the shell was returned Mr Paterson felt he owed it to the world to broadcast his beliefs, no matter how great his fear of the camera's thieving eye. The call of the shell had to be answered.

I yawned and gave a sudden shiver; it was very late

101

now, and cold, but that was not the only reason. Already our lives were changed since that time in the gallery when I had first seen Mr Paterson. What more was to come? I remembered the words he had spoken in court:

> *Not in a green shade does contentment stay,*
> *But in the touch of the apple tree's primeval bark*
> *We find excitement's brilliant way*
> *Into the dark.*

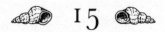 15

Having got Mr Paterson's agreement to appear on his programme, Antony Beaton lost no time in getting to work. There was to be a short film, followed by a five-minute live interview to sum everything up.

'Television is the new reality. A single image on the screen is worth a thousand words,' explained Antony – we were on Christian name terms now. 'Your friend should not be too displeased with such publicity.'

'I suppose not.'

'You sound uncertain. Why is that?' But he supplied his own answer. 'You are wondering what really made him change his mind?'

'In a way.' I could not rid myself of a sense of disappointment, a feeling that somehow we were betrayed, and I said as much. Antony Beaton considered me gravely.

'Don't feel like that, William. There's no need. Something happened to change his mind, that's all.'

'The shell came back,' I said. He shook his head.

'That's not all. I've been watching him these last few days. He is a man acting on instructions. And don't worry, we have his image on the screen, but not his soul.

Believe me, I know about these things.'

'You're probably right,' I agreed reluctantly.

But Antony Beaton hadn't finished. 'He said something I didn't understand at the time, and I hoped you might explain.'

'If I can.'

'He talked about the eyes of the forest and how he must face them and not be afraid. I asked him what he meant by that, but he just said all would be explained in the end.'

I laughed a little bitterly. 'That sounds like the Mr Paterson I know.' But I remembered as I spoke that I had heard those words before.

It was the third day's filming and we were standing outside the fisherman's cottage, grouped rather uneasily together awaiting instructions as to how to appear natural. We were to re-enact our meeting with Mr Paterson and our invitation to tea. To make things even more embarrassing, a crowd had collected to watch, and although they kept a discreet distance, controlled by a somewhat irritable cameraman, I was appallingly conscious of their interested eyes. Ros was not happy either, and looked stiff and tense. They had dressed her in an ankle-length dress instead of her jeans, and had plaited bits of her hair so that she looked like an illustration from *The Lady of Shalott*; I could see the effect they were aiming at. Only Minnie was really at ease. They had chopped an inch or two off her dark curls so she looked more like a sprite than ever, and she seemed not to care about the cameras at all. We had already been through the background bit: a scene in my dark room, and a shot of Ros playing Mendelssohn on the sea shore, and Minnie galloping on poor old Greylag, who was covered in sweat at so many re-takes, although the riding school was probably pleased with all that free publicity. I dreaded to think how we were going to appear; dreamlike or nightmarish, depending on how you looked at us. Mr Paterson, on the other hand, seemed in control of things. Except for insisting on the dark glasses for all camera work and an absolute refusal ever to relinquish the shell, he, like Minnie, appeared unconcerned.

His speech to us about his beliefs came out strong and true, and I could see that the producer was impressed. But it was not all so easy to capture. Mr Paterson refused to blow the shell or make any serious attempt to call either basking sharks or dolphins. Not that it mattered. I overheard Antony Beaton talking about a bit of cross-cutting and 'taking a leaf out of David Attenborough's book'. And there were eye witness accounts of the real happenings. The old salt at the harbour was a natural and did a lot of very effective gazing out to sea while he made enigmatic remarks about the call of the ocean and the secrets of the deep. He had the eyes for that kind of thing. He even consented to smoke a pipe kindly provided by the company, though I had never seen him with anything but a cigarette in his mouth. And the weather was amazingly kind, too, providing sun and clear blue skies, although there was some rain in the evenings. But not too much. There was even one fine windy night for the storm scenes. We were all being manipulated with consummate skill.

Of course, there was an interesting side to all this. I learnt more about photography than I thought possible. One of the crew advised me about my camera and I knew that soon I would be able to afford a new, really good one. Antony had assured us that Mercia Television was generous with its funds. But the sense of unease would not leave me. Perhaps one should never try to recreate the past. Perhaps Mr Paterson was right, and the camera really did steal away one's soul. I was very glad when it was all over.

To mark the end of the film-making there was a celebration party at the local pub, where all who had participated were entertained most generously. Even Mrs Brewster managed to look cheerful.

'In stating the opposite point of view,' she assured Mum, 'I put a perspective on Mr Paterson that will surely end this ridiculous adulation. The man's a trouble-maker, no more, no less. And somebody has to speak out on the side of law and order, to make a stand against the disruptive element in our society.' Mum and I exchanged glances as Mrs Brewster waved a hand in the general direction of Mr Paterson who, still in my sun-glasses, was sipping absently at a glass of wine. He looked rather like an Old Testament prophet who had strayed in by mistake from fasting in the desert.

Ros was obviously having a splendid time. She seemed to have grown mysteriously older during the filming. Watching her talking now to two young assistant editors, I saw that they looked at her with open admiration. I think she had forgotten all about Mr Paterson. Minnie, too, was in her element. She hadn't any right to be in a pub, of course, but Antony Beaton could fix anything. I'm afraid fame hadn't done Minnie much good. You would honestly have thought to listen to her that she had discovered Mr Paterson all by herself. As the evening wore on I began to feel more and more out of things and to wish that everything had been as it was, that none of it had happened. Mum saw my face.

'Don't worry, William. Remember, nothing lasts for ever,' she said, smiling encouragingly. You can never deceive my mother.

But now we couldn't walk anywhere without people looking at us. I hated their whispered comments.

'Isn't that the boy who rescued him?'

'That's the mother. The sister's a violinist. No, not the

105

little one. The pretty older one.'

Minnie wouldn't have liked that last remark. There were always people staring at the house, too, and I began to hate everything about our life. Only Mr Paterson seemed unaffected, spending long hours sitting on his rock or walking over the sands. I never heard him blow his shell, except once, very late, when the sound of it came faint yet clear on the night wind. He had about him an air of confidence. I knew that this had nothing to do with the film or the publicity. It was something else. But what? I turned things over and over in my mind, unable to rid myself of the conviction that there was something waiting in the wings of our crowded stage and that only when the moment was right would it come striding on to face us all.

The day for the showing of the film came at last and we stayed in all evening, but Mr Paterson, who had the live interview at the end, was swept away from us in a large chauffeur-driven car. We waved to him as he drove past. The programme was not until nearly ten o'clock and by then Minnie was pretending not to yawn. We were tense with anxiety. Mum had made a lovely supper, but we could hardly eat a thing. We did the washing up in silence and then wandered restlessly around the house until it was time to switch on.

As it turned out, we needn't have worried. Although I hadn't realised it at the time, Antony Beaton was a real artist at his job. The film was stunningly effective. He had made the most of a marvellous subject. Haunting seascapes, the dreamy charm of the countryside and the empty sands. And through it all, Mr Paterson, strange and wise, yet curiously remote. Whether motionless on his mist-swathed rock, which must have been photographed very early in the morning, or emerging tall and wild from the fisherman's cottage, he looked like a man seeing the first dawn of time. As if only he held the secret of the meaning of life. The harbour scene was well done, the cross-cutting to a scene of plunging dolphins skilful, even if it hadn't really happened like that. I came out quite well myself there, and the old salt was most impressive and spoke more sense than I had realised. The background music was haunting and muted. There was a blurred artistic shot of Ros playing her violin, a wonderfully absorbed expression on her face.

'That's not me playing. That's Yehudi Menuhin,' she said, looking rather annoyed.

If Mr Paterson's statement of his beliefs seemed both affecting and true, Mrs Brewster's condemnation of anything that did not fit into her rigid pattern of behaviour came out as hectoring and false.

'Poor thing. She can't have known what she was letting herself in for.' Mum was always prepared to give that woman the benefit of the doubt.

Other opinions were carefully balanced, both for and against Mr Paterson. But most took the view that he should be allowed to follow his chosen path in peace, and there was even a hint of envy at someone who had so clear a vision. Only one sour fisherman struck a discordant note, complaining about his shattered nets the day the dolphins had come to Northburgh harbour.

But in the end all was tranquillity. The screen showed a long-lens shot of the prophet alone by the shore, holding out his hands to his own mysterious deity. The music swelled and died, leaving only the sounds of the wind and the sea as the beguiling image faded and was gone.

Mum broke into spontaneous applause, and Minnie joined her. Ros sat quietly, though she looked quite pleased. I felt nothing except a huge relief that it was all over and that we'd come out of it unscathed. But I had forgotten about the last live minutes of the programme, which Antony Beaton was now explaining were about to begin. The camera homed in on Mr Paterson, balanced rather precariously on a modern-looking chair set against a blue sky background. His eyes were invisible behind the dark glasses.

Antony Beaton began gently enough. He commended Mr Paterson's individuality and said that in an age in which we were all becoming as alike as the proverbial peas in a pod we should treasure like gold those who listened to a different drum.

'I wish he'd get to the point,' grumbled Minnie, who was looking a bit bored now that she was no longer on the screen.

'Be quiet, Min,' said Mum. 'He'll get there soon enough.'

And now Antony Beaton was leaning forward earnestly. 'This theory of yours about our failure to listen to the voices of the old world is very attractive. You saw in the film how people responded to you; you must find that most encouraging.'

For a moment I thought Mr Paterson was not going to answer, but then he shook his head and said, almost tonelessly, 'I find it neither encouraging nor discouraging. What people think of me is of no interest.'

'But surely that can't be true. After all, a prophet must have his followers.'

'My footsteps are in sand; the tide washes them away.'

That was rather impressive, but Antony Beaton was not a man to be deceived by clever words.

'With respect, may I suggest to you, Adrian – may I call you Adrian?'

'Oh lord, now he's going to be rude,' said Mum anxiously.

'You may not,' Mr Paterson said crisply.

But Antony continued unabashed. 'I suggest to you that this is no more than an attractive fairytale, a harmless deception. You have no job, nor any proper home, so you have chosen a gullible rural community on which to try out your ideas for self-publicity. What do you say to that?' The voice was soft, pleasant, belying the stabbing words.

Mr Paterson merely smiled, as if he had been expecting just this question. 'I came to Northburgh because it is a place at the edge, though whether of darkness or of light I do not yet know. The gods will declare themselves in their own way.'

For a moment Antony Beaton seemed at a loss for words. He fidgeted with his spectacles and I could see the beads of sweat on his forehead. Then, with a slight smile, he said, 'But we are not gods, Mr Paterson. We are mortals. And mortals need proof.'

Mr Paterson gave a deep sigh, as if no less wearied and exasperated by the conversation than by the limitations of mere mortals. But his answer when it came was simple enough. 'If it's proof you want that the old world lives, I can give it to you.'

The meaning of the words took several seconds to sink in, but then Antony Beaton laughed deprecatingly. 'Come now. That's quite a statement. But can you substantiate it?'

For the first time Mr Paterson looked directly at us from the screen. The fierce eyes were impenetrable behind the black lenses.

'No. He mustn't. He's going too far,' Ros cried, though whether she meant Mr Paterson or Antony Beaton I wasn't sure. Minnie moved so close to the television, she was practically in it. For an interminable time Mr Paterson said nothing.

'Well? What is your answer? All the viewers are on

109

tenterhooks to know.'

'I repeat, I can give you proof, if that is what you want.'

'Then,' said Antony Beaton in a low, intense voice, 'I challenge you to call up a creature from the old world.'

'Oh my God,' whispered Mum.

But Antony Beaton had not finished. 'Living proof, no moonshine, in the clear light of day.'

'And where will you find me such a creature?' Mr Paterson's voice was without expression. It was impossible to tell what he was thinking.

'I can tell you that now.' Antony Beaton spoke slowly, as though determined that his listeners should catch every syllable. 'It is a creature that up to now has eluded all attempts – and there have been many – to discover it. My challenge to you is to summon up the so-called monster from Loch Ness.'

'Then I shall do just that. I accept your challenge,' said Mr Paterson, as if it were the most obvious thing in the world.

There was a stunned silence. For once even Antony Beaton was too taken aback to speak, and, the time having run out, the picture faded like a dream before our astonished eyes.

Mum groaned. 'What on earth got into Antony Beaton?' she asked. 'I never thought he'd be so irresponsible.'

'Mr Paterson's done it now,' cried Minnie. She sounded more pleased than concerned.

'No one will ever take him seriously after this,' said Ros.

'Yes, they will,' Minnie insisted. 'Mr Paterson can do anything he wants.'

I ignored Minnie and looked first at Ros, then at Mum. 'I'm not so sure,' I said slowly. 'He has such complete belief in what he's doing, who are we to say that he's wrong?'

Mum shook her head, but Ros said, 'Who indeed? Only I don't know if he should have said what he did.'

'He'll do it. You'll see.' Minnie kept repeating it over and over again until Mum sent her up to bed. I wished I could share her comfortable certainty.

 16

What happened next is best described by a picture I once saw in an old-fashioned children's book and have never been quite able to forget: Pandora had opened the forbidden box, and round the cringing, terrified little girl flew a cloud of winged insects and dreadful shapes of the world's evil. Mr Paterson had opened the box called 'Media' and round his head flew tormenting images, while voices cried and questioned endlessly: 'Why are you doing that? What does it mean? Are you sane? Can you prove it? Tell us. Speak to us.' On and on without a break. But he bore it all with the same detachment we had witnessed before. He remained silent, ignoring the laughter and disbelief, the scorn, the dismissive remarks. And not all were sceptical. Could he really do this thing? Had he really got some strange power? There were more things in heaven and earth . . .

To give him his due, Antony Beaton was really concerned. He came to see us a few days after the programme.

'I don't know if we should have issued such a challenge.' He spread his fingers wide as if letting all responsibility slip through them like sand.

'Would you have stopped him if you'd known he'd accept?' asked Mum.

'Mrs Seaward, we like to think that we in the media are not entirely heartless. I have certainly warned him about the publicity. Can he stand it, that's what I want to know?

111

This type of thing can be very overwhelming, particularly to someone totally unused to it.' He looked distressed and at that moment I liked him more than I had ever done. He continued. 'And what about the intrepid Seaward family?'

'Not too bad. Just a few reporters and the telephone rings rather a lot. Mr Paterson won't speak to anyone, you see. They want to get it out of the children.' Mum sounded cross.

'They would, they would.'

'And I am a bit worried about the effect on Ros's scholarship. Too much publicity could surely be a bad thing.'

Antony Beaton buried his head in his hands. 'Don't go on, please. I've just survived a visit to Mrs Brewster and was looking to this house as a kind of haven. And then you tell me there's a storm at sea.'

We all laughed, but rather uneasily.

After he had gone I went over to the window and looked out. Far below on his rock sat Mr Paterson, watched by a small but inquisitive crowd. We had tried to speak to him, but since the broadcast he seemed to have shut us off. It was rather hurtful in a way, but Mum told Minnie that prophets could be selfish when it came to pursuing their beliefs. I watched him walk back to his cottage, the advancing tide wiping away his footsteps as if he had never passed that way.

But it wasn't like that, for the next thing we heard was that Mr Paterson was to appear on *Nationwide*, linking in to the main programme from the Mercian studios.

'He can't know what he's doing. He'll cease to be just local. He'll be seen by the whole country,' I said to Mum.

She said I had left things too long and must try to stop him now. But I was too late. By the time I reached Mr Paterson, a car had already picked him up and was driving him away. As he smiled at me and waved a gracious hand he looked like a man who hadn't a care in the world.

On my return I found Mum with a glass of wine in her hand. She hadn't done that for ages. She gave Ros and me a glass each and Minnie had a Coke.

'You're not having wine, even if you did make a film,' she said firmly.

There was a trailer for the programme just before the early evening news. 'In tonight's *Nationwide* we bring you news of a new find in the North Sea, a well-known face bows out of the political race and the man who claims he can call up the Loch Ness monster with a shell.'

We couldn't bear to watch it and switched off the set, preferring to sit in gloomy silence, sipping our drinks.

But of course Antony Beaton rang and told us all about it. Apparently the *Nationwide* team had assembled a battery of experts from the Natural History Museum, amateurs with blurred film clips and underwater divers who had all declared such a feat impossible. There had been a great deal of good-natured chaff, and through it all Mr Paterson had sat unmoved. An extraordinary man with an extraordinary claim, as they said. He would go to Loch Ness as he had been challenged and planned to travel to Scotland at the end of the week.

After that Mr Paterson was the darling of the media. I'm not a newsman, but I could see the attraction. A human story with elements of fantasy and hope, as well as the strong possibility of entertaining farce. In a world of disbelief and harsh everyday facts, the prophet in his bizarre dress, with his enigmatic face and eyes permanently hidden behind dark glasses, attracted maximum coverage. I can't think that anyone could really have believed in it all, yet I had a feeling of such unreality that I was sure I was living in a dream from which I would soon awake. Somehow I must get him to talk. There must

113

be an answer to all this, and I was convinced I was the only one to find out.

He was alone, for once, and sitting on the shingle when I found him.

'I'm glad you've come. I've something to show you,' he said. We went into the cottage and I saw that he had been trying to remove the shells from the walls. Many were chipped and broken. 'I'm afraid I underestimated the qualities of Superglue,' he told me sadly.

'You didn't have to do it,' I exclaimed. 'You didn't really have to answer that challenge. It was only meant to be a joke. These television people can be very stupid and irresponsible sometimes.'

'The old world has spoken.'

'No, no,' I cried. 'The gods don't ask you to sacrifice yourself in front of millions of people.'

'It is because of the eyes, William, that I go,' he said quietly.

That phrase again. *The eyes of the forest*. But what did it mean?

'Mr Paterson, please, I don't understand.'

He shook his head, but he had taken off the sun-glasses and the green eyes were kind. 'You are the best and only friends I ever had, you and your sisters. Perhaps especially you, William.' As he spoke he picked absently at the sharp edges of the broken shells. I tried to help in the impossible task of levering them off the walls. I didn't know any more what to say, so I just helped for a bit.

Later, he walked with me to the rocks to say goodbye and as he stood on the shingle, his arms raised in farewell, it came to me that I couldn't let him go alone to face the challenge. Friends did not desert each other in their hour of need. Old-fashioned, you may think, but that's how I felt. Stopping, I looked back. His voice came to me on the wind, faint yet clear.

114

'Don't forget your camera, William.' I don't know how he knew that I was going to go with him. But he did, just as he had always known that the gods would answer in their own good time and in their own inscrutable way.

The problem, of course, was Mum. 'You can't possibly go to Scotland,' she said flatly. 'I can't allow it. In any case, you haven't any money.'

'*Please*. Nothing like this will ever happen again.'

'But you can't believe in any of this, William. You can't.'

I searched for the right words. 'We can't just abandon him. We're his friends, all of us . . .'

Mum ran a hand wearily over her forehead. 'Oh I don't know. If your father were here, he'd know what to do.'

'He'd say we were doing the right thing. I know he would.'

She looked at me, and there were unfamiliar tears in her eyes. 'Would he? Oh William, you're all I've got. And I do so rely on you. I always will.'

'Then you know why I must go.'

Mum gave in then.

When Ros heard she refused to be left out. Mum protested, but Ros can be very stubborn when she chooses. 'All right,' Mum told her. 'You two can go, but not Minnie. She's far too young.'

I won't go into the fuss that Minnie made, which was the worst I had ever heard, even from her. That so small a child could make so much noise was almost unbelievable. Suffice it to say that in the end she was allowed to go, Antony Beaton having agreed to be responsible for her safety.

Only Mum refused to come. 'Someone must take care of things here,' she explained. 'Besides, I can't just leave the shop at a moment's notice.' But I thought the real reason was that she was sure Mr Paterson would fail, and she couldn't bear to see it.

Minnie, of course, had no such doubts. Her small face burned with excitement and her dark eyes were alight with indestructible faith. And as the day of our departure drew nearer, something of her enthusiasm seemed to infect Ros and me. Nevertheless, I found time amidst all our feverish preparations to buy an excellent new camera, which had a built-in flash and other refinements. Minnie took over my old one without asking, but I hadn't the heart to tell her off.

Mum looked tired and anxious by the time we were ready to leave. But all she said was 'Take care,' as we loaded our bags into the hired car that had been ordered to get us to the airport. I looked back before we turned out of sight of the house, but she had disappeared inside.

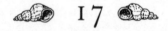 17

I have difficulty now in recalling much of our journey, except that Mr Paterson seemed to enjoy himself and laid the shell on a spare seat beside him. We came down through the clouds to Inverness Airport at about four o'clock in the afternoon, and even before we landed I could see the waiting crowd. I was thankful when the cars whisked us away to our destination, but Minnie took it all very much in her stride.

'I've never stayed at a proper hotel before. And all paid for,' she kept saying. I wished that she would be quiet.

It was no better at the hotel either. The crush was awful, and I heard the babble of other languages; foreign news teams were there as well. There was even a man in a kilt who was busy telling anyone who would listen that he

watched the Loch every day for a sign of the monster.
The thought grew in my mind like a dark cloud that if Mr
Paterson was to fail in front of all these people and the
countless viewing millions, it would be our fault. We had
got him into this. We had told him about the Triton shell.
We had given him Neptune's horn. Yet amidst it all Mr
Paterson seemed untroubled and perfectly at peace with
himself. I marvelled that he could be like that, knowing
what tomorrow might bring.

We did not go to bed until very late that night, but
watched television in our rooms until the myriad whirl-
ing images made my head ache. It was aching still when I
woke to a bright, clear morning. We had a late breakfast
and then set off in a convoy of vehicles to the television's
chosen place on the Loch. This turned out to be the ruins
of Urquhart Castle, beautifully situated on a small,
wooded promontory. Although destroyed by fire in the
seventeenth century, the castle still had sufficient form to
be an impressive setting for such an enterprise as this.
Apparently, too, there had once been a sighting here,
and a blurred photograph of what might have been a
submerged creature travelling at speed was to be found
in the guide book I had bought at the hotel.

It was still relatively early but already the cameramen
were perched like crows on walls and archways, even on
the castle's ruined tower. If there was to be anything to be
seen, no one was going to miss it. Certainly not the
fair-sized crowd of eager holiday makers in whose midst
an enterprising salesman of china models of the monster
and every kind of tartan souvenir had set up a makeshift
stall. The more I saw, the less I liked what was happening. And the amused presence of a famous nature artist
did nothing to lessen my sense of unease and embarrassment.

Our arrival was greeted with a scatter of ironic

applause. Against her will, Ros had been persuaded to put on her long dress and to plait her hair the way it had been in the film. She looked wan and nervous, and even Minnie had dark circles under her eyes. But we allowed ourselves to be photographed as the Seaward family, friends and followers of Northburgh's prophet, fish-caller extraordinary. And if we were upset by all this, Mr Paterson seemed perfectly calm, though we could no longer see his eyes behind the dark glasses.

I saw Antony Beaton in the distance, but he appeared to be too deep in discussion with one of his camera crew to come over to see us. Or perhaps he was beginning to be as embarrassed as I was. Nor was the *Northburgh News* left out. Martin Parker was there, although there was no sign of his cameraman.

The morning wore on, but Mr Paterson seemed in no hurry to begin. He wasted endless time brewing up some of his horrible tea over a borrowed camping stove and polishing the Triton shell with a dirty handkerchief. One of the reporters told us he was to make two attempts to call up the monster, one in the early part of the day and one in the late afternoon. It seemed to depend on the angle of the sun, though I couldn't really see what that had to do with it.

Eventually Antony Beaton made his way over to us. He seemed cheerful enough, but I detected a flash of anxiety in his eyes. 'I'll want to film you all together,' he told us, 'and then of course, at the end, Mr Paterson on his own.' He did not specify what he thought 'the end' might be. There were to be no interviews, he said, not until after the event. 'No disturbance, my dears. Everyone calm and peaceful until the great moment.' And he hurried away before I had time to answer.

Minnie was beginning to get very bored and restless, but she didn't leave my side. A cameraman lent Ros a coat to put over her dress; there were clouds in the sky now and a chilly wind blew off the Loch. I began to think that time had stopped. But at last Mr Paterson, who had been sitting on the grass with his arms round the shell, stood up and announced in his strange, harsh voice that he was ready for the first attempt.

There was a narrow shingle beach just beneath the castle walls, which would serve perfectly for his purpose. Mr Paterson walked slowly down to the water's edge while the cameras recorded every step of his lonely way. He had taken off the cloak and was dressed only in his robe. Someone must have given it a wash, for he looked ghostly white and unearthly in the fleeting sunshine. The Loch was never still, the wind stroked the surface into endless ripples which hurt your eyes if you looked too long. Farther out, a flotilla of boats rode at anchor. Batteries of infra red and sonar equipment waited by the small jetty on the other side of the castle. There was a murmur of excited anticipation. Like an actor waiting for the audience to settle, Mr Paterson stood motionless until a complete, expectant silence ovewhelmed the watchers.

'I feel sick,' whispered Minnie as, slowly and elegantly, like a true prophet, Mr Paterson raised the Triton shell to his lips and blew. Very gently at first, then louder and louder across the expanse of water. But the sound that came from the shell was not the one we knew. I glanced at Ros. She was frowning and did not move or look at me. Again he blew, an oddly muffled and unaffecting note. Even the rhythm was different, faster and jerky, with no real pattern.

'He's doing it all wrong,' Minnie hissed, voicing our thoughts.

'Hush,' said someone. 'You'll put him off.'

Again Mr Paterson raised the shell and again the muffled notes sounded, but so faintly now that you could

119

hardly hear them. Then he sat down.

We waited and waited, in dead silence, not wishing to break the spell. Nothing happened. The grey surface of the Loch was as cold and unyielding as polished steel. Someone suggested that there had to be a time lapse because the Loch was twenty miles long and nobody knew how deep. The minutes passed with agonising slowness as Mr Paterson sat alone and silent at the water's edge.

'It's time for this caper to end,' said a cameraman. 'Then we can all go and get a decent drink. It's all this God-forsaken spot has to offer.'

'I know it's the silly season, but this is ridiculous,' grumbled another.

I frowned at them, but you couldn't really blame them. They were bored and fed up with waiting for something – anything – to happen. Nevertheless I kept my own camera at the ready and whiled away some time helping Minnie with hers. Ros seemed disinterested. 'I'd rather just look,' she said. I think Ros had given the monster up, for this time at least.

It was getting colder and a few drops of rain began to fall. The holiday makers put on anoraks and plastic mackintoshes and huddled in the lee of the castle walls. Some drifted off to their cars while the camera crews stood about in groups, smoking endless cigarettes. We ate the few sandwiches we had brought with us, and then sat together, willing the time to pass quickly.

If anything, the afternoon seemed longer and more tedious than the morning had been. The wind had got up and the showers of rain came more and more frequently. An air of depression settled over the watchers. But at last it was time for the second attempt. Again Mr Paterson stood up. In spite of his earlier failure and the rain, which had soaked his hair and cloak, he had lost none of his

oked at it in silence. Then, over
cried, 'So that's why the monste
n't hear you properly!'
hat was bothering me. 'No on
e without a reason. But you neve
d.

Ros stooped to pick up the tissue
use they tried to make a fool o

was completely loyal. 'You won'
will be all right next time.'
'm glad, Miranda, to see you have
.'

at you did today?' I had to know
y to explain,' he answered doubt-

s.

Mr Paterson didn't answer. When
vords very carefully.
est where man first walked there
he forest was full of predators, the
beasts. A man's life was brief and
ain. But he was not defeated. He
e weapons and a fire to keep away
en his darkness.' He paused, and
reflective way.
with what you did today?' I asked.
ee the forest, but the watching eyes
, shining, indestructible eyes. Ever
ferate as we breathe.' I was begin-

d Ros.
odern world – lenses, telescopes,
satellites, electronic devices. Every
us. A thousand times more deadly

commanding presence. He seemed composed, even cheerful. Once or twice he turned round to look at the waiting crowd, and there was an expression on his face that was impossible to interpret. Again he raised the shell and again the notes sounded strange and muffled. Nothing happened, and I saw one of the directors shake his head. He was not looking at all happy; I suppose he had to compose an epitaph for all his hopes and reckon up the enormous bill which there must have been for such a junket.

Again and again the shell sounded in the unresponsive air. I have been in a good many distressing and embarrassing situations in my life, but I can tell you that nothing, absolutely nothing, has ever surpassed that day at Loch Ness. I still grow cold when I think of it.

'Why doesn't the monster come?' Minnie was desolate, her small face pinched and grey beneath the dark, dripping curls. I put my arm round her.

'Listen, Min, I don't think there's going to be any monster. We shouldn't be here, any of us.'

'No monster!' Her voice rose. 'Of course there's a monster. I'm just tired of waiting, that's all.' And she jerked away from me.

'You're right, Miranda. There is a monster. We made our own,' said a voice behind us and I swung round to see Antony Beaton. He was wearing a tartan hat in a half-hearted way and there was a bottle of whisky sticking out of his pocket. His voice was slightly slurred, but what he said was true. We had conjured up a monster, a creation of exploitation, gullibility and greed, and it was here at the edge of the Loch, neck outstretched, savage mouth wide, to devour poor lonely deranged Mr Paterson. I felt a sense of shame I had not known before.

The rain was falling without mercy now. Someone began to slow-handclap and there were a few jeers and some unkind laughter, quickly quelled, only to rise again. I couldn't tell if it was the rain on their cheeks or if Ros and Minnie were really crying, but I knew one thing for certain: Mr Paterson must be made to bring this dreadful charade to an end. The onlookers were getting angry. I could bear it no longer. Heedless of shouts and bursting free from restraining hands, I dashed down the now slippery green slope and half fell, half slid to the beach beside him. He gave no sign that he had noticed my abrupt arrival.

'Come away, please, Mr Paterson. It hasn't worked and it's not going to. You know that. I know that. Come on before we all get pneumonia. It was a good try. It really was.'

He stood quite still without saying anything. I feared to look at his face. Then suddenly he began to laugh, as he had done that night on the hill. Laughing and laughing until he nearly dropped the shell.

I was appalled. 'They'll think you're laughing at them. You're probably on camera. They'll think you're making a fool of them. Or you've gone mad.' I ran out of things they might think.

For an instant he laid a cold hand on mine. 'Have no fear, William, have no fear. I shall do as you ask.'

He said no more, but he was still laughing as we climbed the slope together. Once or twice I glanced back. If monster there was, the call of the Triton had failed to wake him from his primeval sleep.

Yet there was something puzzling about the whole affair, that did not fit the pattern. I wanted to ask Mr Paterson about it, but he was hurried away to be interviewed. I would have to await my opportunity.

I would like to draw a veil over the rest of that evening. Mr Paterson gave a number of cheerful interviews about

than the animals of the forest. And now we have no fire. Nor are they afraid, because they have no heart.'

'But if we can't make a fire, how shall we keep them away?' asked Minnie fearfully.

'That's the difficulty. A very great difficulty.'

'But that can't be the end of it.'

'No, William, it is not. We must remember who we truly are and light a fire with our imaginations. We must think back to the time when we were free and there were no false images to betray us. I wanted to show that if we choose, we can defeat the images that confuse and betray our natural senses. I wanted the image makers to be duped and mocked, because others will follow my example. If we cannot go forward, we will go back. The horizon is made of steel and we cannot cross. We must return to the forest from whence we came. The pathways are always there, but you have to clear the weeds and shine a light into the dark. Music is one such light, as I think you know, Rosalind.' Ros smiled.

But I was remembering back to that evening in the shell house. *It is because of the eyes*, he had said. I understood at last, but now it seemed a thousand years ago.

There was much more that I wanted to know, but our brief moment of privacy was at an end. There was a buzz of voices in the corridor outside, calling for Mr Paterson.

'Don't go, don't go,' pleaded Minnie.

'They are angry because they know that they have no power over me.' And he held out his hands towards us, saying in a gentle voice, 'Come now, my friends, and we will face our critics together.'

Those whom the gods destroy, they first make mad, I thought sadly.

18

The mood of the crowd still gathered in the hotel that evening was in marked contrast to that which had prevailed throughout the day. The television people had well and truly drowned their sorrows, but behind their apparent cheerfulness there was no sense of anticipation. Useless to say they had expected too much, that they had built the whole grotesque edifice and now that their house of cards had fallen they blamed the faces on the paste-board for its destruction. Only the experts seemed relieved that nothing had happened, that their industry of informed speculation could continue uninterrupted. The myths survived, the legend lived. They much preferred it that way.

We did our best, but there wasn't much to say. Wary of curious stares and difficult questions, we eventually slipped upstairs to my room, glad to escape the raucous laughter in the bar.

'I never realised people could be so cruel,' said Ros.

'You have to win; they like you then,' said Minnie, quite profoundly really.

We didn't feel like going to bed, so we talked until Minnie fell asleep in the chair. I was restless. I pulled aside the curtain to look out. The rain had stopped. The moon was high and silver in a cloudless sky. I glanced at my watch. It was after eleven.

'Who is he really, Ros?'

Ros shook her head. She was unplaiting her hair. 'I don't know. I don't think we'll ever know.'

'Do you think he'll come back to Northburgh after this?'

We looked at each other without speaking because we had no answer.

126

At that moment there was a knock on the door. We didn't answer at first, but the knock came again. Who could want to see us at this time of night?

'Come in,' said Ros, wearily.

The door opened. Mr Paterson stood on the threshold, wearing our father's cloak. An old sack was over his back and he held the shell in the crook of his arm.

'You look ready to . . .' I couldn't finish the sentence.

'They're all in the bar. They won't notice us go.'

'Go? Where?'

Mr Paterson didn't answer that. Instead he said, 'Can you all come quickly. There's no time to waste.'

'Come with you? Where?' I still didn't understand.

'Don't you know?'

'Look, Mr Paterson, we're all exhausted. Can't you leave it till the morning?'

At the sound of our raised voices Minnie stirred, and woke. 'Is it now?' she asked, sitting up, rubbing her eyes.

'Yes,' said Mr Paterson.

'But where are we going in the middle of the night?'

'Oh, William, you can be so stupid,' said Minnie scornfully.

There was no more time to argue. Besides we were too tired. And something inside me stirred excitedly. 'All right, we'll come,' I said.

Minnie and Ros went off to their room to collect jumpers and coats. I put on everything warm that I possessed and picked up my camera. When Minnie returned I noticed that she had my old Brownie slung round her neck.

We had little difficulty going downstairs. A chambermaid gave us a curious look, but, as Mr Paterson had said, everyone else was in the bar. We stole through the revolving doors. There was a car parked nearby and our luck was in, the keys were inside.

'I think this is Antony Beaton's car,' said Ros.

'He won't mind. He's nice,' said Minnie.

I felt a momentary pang because he was nice. I got in the front with Mr Paterson, the others sat behind.

I don't know where Mr Paterson learnt to drive, but I'm sure it must have been a very long time ago. He ground the gears painfully, swerving first one way, then the next. I cannot imagine how the police ever missed us, but at last we were outside the city.

None of us asked where we were going now because we knew. Mr Paterson was going to try again.

Mr Paterson drew the car to the side of the road some distance from the Loch and we got out and stood looking over the moonlit water. We knew where we were, yet it was a different place. The trees cast dark shadows on the road and the hills were black against the glittering sky.

'Perfect,' said Mr Paterson, 'absolutely perfect.' And he strode away along the road towards the castle ruin, dark and formidable. We followed a little distance behind. There was a sharpness in the air, but the cold we felt was not from that.

We turned through the gate and down the grass slope.

'Do you think we have to go right down to the beach?' whispered Minnie. 'We could see all right from here.'

No one answered her. Mr Paterson paused and waited for us to catch him up.

'Are you afraid, Mr Paterson?' asked Minnie.

'If you're not then I'm not,' he answered calmly.

So Minnie stiffened her shoulders in a brave effort to banish her fear, and ran on ahead down the dewy grass to the shingle beach. Against the silver reflection of the moon, the water looked dark and deep, flat calm, shining, a mirror for the eyes of the universe.

We followed Minnie to the Loch's edge and stood together, yet separate, in our thoughts, waiting for the

128

unthinkable. Slowly, carefully, Mr Paterson raised the shell to his lips and we fixed our gaze on the moonlit distance. This time the sound that came from the shell was more beautiful than anything I had ever heard. It seemed to run through my body, sharp as pain. A single call, no complex rhythm; just one long note, then another and another. Irresistible, cold and piercing to the consciousness like the winter wind.

I don't know how long we stood there, feeling the seconds pass with our beating hearts. At last Mr Paterson put down the shell. We waited. A tiny moonlit ripple broke like a miniature wave on our pebbly shore. And then another. Mr Paterson motioned sharply for us to go back a little and I felt Minnie's hand grip my jacket. Ros stepped a few paces behind me and, like a wary animal, stood poised for flight. My fingers touched the leather strap of the camera. I felt the outline of the lens and the sharp, cold hardness of the shutter. I held my breath, fearing that the sound of it would break the spell. Absolute stillness; even the owls were mute. Mr Paterson raised his arm and pointed. I could only see his face in profile, but I heard the sharp intake of his breath.

'Get your camera ready!'

Minnie released her hold on my jacket. I focused the lens and strained my eyes into the night. At the same time my ears caught a distant rushing-water sound, like a boat at speed. Louder, louder, nearer and nearer. A swooping wind tore at our clothes and the waters of the Loch swirled into violent life, leaping against the shore. I shivered in the sudden cold and struggled to hold the camera steady, to calm my reeling senses. I glanced at Ros, who stood watching, very still and quiet, curiously unafraid. Minnie clung tightly to me.

Now we were drowning in a rushing torrent of sound. I stared out across that black, heaving surface and I saw, coming towards me very fast from the centre of the Loch, a swimming, moonlit creature, an undulating snaking thing with a wake of glittering foam. A bank of water overwhelmed the shore and I leapt back, dragging Minnie with me. The force of my terror made me strong.

Then something huge beyond belief reared up higher, higher than a crane, blotting out the moon. The dripping skin, black as dragon's wings, was runnelled, grooved as a rock or an ancient tree. It was risen from the dark, wearing the icy mantle of the deep and a crown of stars. The king of a far country. I was numb with shock and fear, yet somehow I managed to press the camera's shutter and the exploding flash aureoled a vast snake's head. In that second I stared into the fathomless eyes and saw Time look back at me, and I knew myself to be falling . . . falling into an endless void.

But Minnie, brave Minnie, tore me from Time's grasp. I felt her frantic tug on my jacket, lost my balance, staggered back and we fell together on to the soaking grass. I looked up.

Now there was the dreadful scrape of leathery skin on the pebbly shore, the bitter breath and the aching, aching cold from the bottom of the world. I thought I heard Mr Paterson cry out then, a wild, exultant cry, and in that instant the beast turned back. But at the water's edge it stopped. I held my breath. I could see it clearly now. The mighty arched back, jagged-edged like a giant saw, cut into the glittering night. Awesome, majestic, indestructible as the old gods; yet beautiful, mysterious as Mr Paterson's elusive dream. A creature of myth made real, moonshine on its scaly hide.

My terror was changed suddenly to wonder, and a wild excitement ran like quicksilver through my blood. I saw the beast lower its encrusted head, stoop its massive body. There was a crack like a huge whip and the lashing tail

130

passed so close I could feel the wind of it on my cheek. Then I heard a deep plunge and we were drenched in freezing spray. I stumbled to my feet, wiping the blinding drops from my eyes. But it had gone. The shore was empty. The king had returned to his far country, and only a spreading silver arrow on the surface of the Loch marked his passing.

I stared over the water until the last ripple was no more. The silence was so intense that it was almost audible, and the shining eye of the Loch looked up in ancient recognition at the unforgiving moon. Behind me, Minnie lay whimpering on the grass. Ros had covered her face with her hands. But of Mr Paterson there was no sign. He had vanished silently, absolutely, into the night.

 19

When I think back on those next few minutes that seemed like hours, they are all jumbled and confused in my mind. I remember the cold, the wet grass, Minnie clinging to me and Ros, stunned and bewildered, shivering so violently that she was forced to sit down. Then the roar of cars approaching, and lights, sirens, people running and torches flashing in our dazzled eyes. Hands helping Ros to her feet, thrusting blankets round our shoulders, and endless questions which we were unable to answer. Except Minnie, who kept crying, 'We saw the monster, we saw it,' over and over again. Then I caught sight of Antony Beaton, agitated and dishevelled.

'You didn't drive . . .' He saw my face. 'What on earth has been happening, William? Where is Mr Paterson?'

The words echoed and echoed in my head. I couldn't answer him; I couldn't speak. There were more voices shouting now, more lights, cars moving away down the road, but no one came to say that Mr Paterson was found. I heard later that they searched everywhere, calling his name. They shouted and shouted, but the echoes sounding over the Loch received no reply.

They took us back to the hotel then, because we were frozen and exhausted. In the morning, they said, they were going to comb the surrounding hills. There was even talk of dragging the Loch, but I knew that was unlikely. A body in those murky waters would be trapped for ever beneath the steep overhanging ledges. But had he drowned? I wiped the damp from the lens of my camera and shut it away in its case. The flash bulb had exploded, there was no mistake about that. I had imagined nothing. *If only I could take just one fantastic photo. A neon flash of fame and fortune* – I closed my eyes against the glare of such a possibility. Mr Paterson's face swam before me. By the time we reached our beds even Minnie was unsure if it had all been no more than a dream, though she was still murmuring something about the moon and monsters and how she hadn't been afraid as she fell asleep.

The search was resumed early the next morning, but we heard no news until almost ten o'clock. And then it was only that nothing had been found, no trace whatsoever of Mr Paterson in the hills around or in the Loch itself. Ros and I were desolate. We didn't know what to do. Our plane wasn't due to leave until late afternoon and we were still shaken and exhausted. We had told no one what we had seen, and Minnie was still asleep. We sat in my room, not wanting to go downstairs.

'We mustn't say anything until we're certain,' I said.

'But Minnie –'

'They'll think she made it up. You know how she embroiders everything.'

132

'I didn't really see the monster,' said Ros, and her voice trembled at the memory. 'Not properly. I couldn't bear to look. I just saw a great dim shape. That's all.' We were silent for a few minutes, each seeing again what we had seen the night before.

'We mustn't speak until we have proof,' I said at last. 'We owe him that at least.'

'Proof? The camera? Oh William, you don't think . . .'

'I don't know. I'll have to wait.' I didn't want to talk about it, and as it happened, I didn't have to because the door opened and Antony Beaton came in.

'I think your little sister is calling. She seems very much awake.' Ros slipped thankfully out of the room.

Antony Beaton sat down on the edge of the bed. He looked oddly subdued and, without his enthusiasm, he seemed to have shrunk. His suede jacket was spotted with rain. He took off his spectacles and wiped them nervously with a silk handkerchief, and I saw that his eyes were strained and shadowed.

'They haven't found him.'

'I know. I expect he'll be all right.' I tried to sound cheerful.

'He wouldn't take any money you know. Not a penny.'

'But I thought . . . for the film and everything . . .'

He shook his head. 'Booked him his air ticket and paid the hotel expenses. That's all we did. Nothing else.'

'But why did he refuse? He needed the money badly after all that had happened.'

Antony Beaton went over to the window where he stood looking out. 'I don't think your Mr Paterson liked me very much.'

I was at a loss for words, but he understood my silence.

'I was really sorry about that, William. He was so wonderfully genuine. In my job you meet so many cranks and phonies; I sometimes think I'm one myself. I wanted to

133

believe in his ideas, but more than that I wanted to believe in him – and I wanted him to believe in me.'

He turned from the window. I couldn't see his eyes. 'Sometimes, William, a figure from one's childhood steps out of the past into the present. If Mr Paterson hadn't existed I could have created him from my imagination. When I was a child, fantasy seemed the only world in which I could believe. When I grew up I learnt to keep quiet and accept reality.' He paused.

I wanted to hear more. 'Please go on.'

He sighed. 'Yesterday, by the Loch, I thought for a moment to see my two worlds become one. That from my childhood imaginings Mr Paterson would call up a mythical, fantastic creature and . . . well, shatter the barriers between fact and fantasy that keep us from our understanding of the world and of each other.'

I longed to confide in him, to tell him what we had seen and the proof I hoped we would have. But I couldn't be sure that he would keep silent, and I dared not risk that. As I hesitated he bent down and picked up my camera from the floor. He examined it closely for a moment.

'You had this with you last night.' The penetrating eyes were on me. 'You wouldn't be holding out on me, William, would you?' I didn't know what to say, so I pretended I did not understand.

'Ah well, on with the motley,' he said, and I could not meet his eyes.

Two hours later, through a storm of unanswered questions and disappointed faces, we made our way to the plane.

I have never been so glad to be home in all my life. Mum was overcome with relief. 'I shouldn't have let you go alone. I should have been there,' she kept saying.

'It's all right,' Ros said soothingly. 'We're all in one

piece. Really.' She did most of the talking that evening, but never once, not even by a look or a careless word, did she betray our secret. Minnie was unusually quiet, which may have been because she was tired out.

The following morning the police came to ask us if we had any idea of Mr Paterson's whereabouts. We could tell them nothing. By the afternoon everyone was beginning to lose interest in the Seaward family. By teatime we were alone at last.

Minnie was nowhere to be seen, so I nodded at Ros to keep Mum entertained and hurried upstairs to my dark room. I went inside, turned on the infra red lamp and shut the door. I undid the camera case and gently rolled on to the end of the film. It was true. I had only taken one exposure.

I heard Minnie's step on the stair. I seized and held the door.

'Keep out, or you'll ruin everything!'

'But I've got a film, too. Won't you develop it with yours? Please, William, please.'

'You didn't take a photograph. You didn't have a flash.'

'I might have done,' she said defensively.

I closed my camera carefully and opened the door a crack. 'Give it to me then and wait out there. Don't move or I'll kill you.' Something in my tone must have impressed my sister. For once, Minnie did as she was told.

And indeed when I looked, she had taken a single exposure, but without a flash; nothing could have come out. I decided to humour her. I set out my trays of solution with sweating hands. Fearful doubts assailed me. Perhaps I should have got a chemist or a professional photographic studio to do the developing. But this was my secret. Something I had to do myself.

I carried out my usual routine. I laid the two exposures

135

in separate trays. Then I locked the door from the inside in case Minnie should change her mind. For a long moment I closed my eyes and prayed. When I opened them again, I stared down at the first tray.

As if from a long distance, out of the mist, an image appeared, blurred and ghostly at first. Then, gradually, as I watched in the red glow of my dark room, the image became clear. I thought my heart would stop. For there in my cloudy sea of chemicals, the monster rose, marvellously alive and wearing a necklace of water drops. Head on, the great eyes shining with the knowledge of a primeval past, the glance of a million years.

'Are you still in there, William?' called an anxious Minnie. I had completely forgotten she was there.

'Wait a minute.' I tried to keep my voice steady. I wanted to be sure. There must be no mistake. I had managed to get in sufficient background to identify the site as Loch Ness. In the bottom right of the picture was Mr Paterson's outstretched arm.

Now I had to believe. I had really done it. I had my fame and fortune here before me in the tiny, close room. I lifted the dripping photograph and placed it with infinite care in a bath of fixative. The monster's eyes stared back, unwavering, through my tears. Now fact and fantasy were one, soaring over the dividing wall on imagination's burning wings.

'What is it, William? What's wrong?' Minnie was hammering on the door.

'Wait. You can't come in. I've got to do your film.'

I doubted whether there would be anything to see. But I was wrong. There was an image on Minnie's film, which for some reason was taking a long time to form. Then, as I watched, astonished, there appeared, rather grey and indistinct, then sharp and splendidly clear, the face of Mr Paterson, smiling his inward smile.

It was impossible. There had been no flash. Minnie hadn't pressed the trigger; I was sure of that. And you were looking the other way. But I knew what you had done, Mr Paterson. You had given me my neon flash of fame, you had given Ros the key to the land she sought, but to Minnie – who had always believed – you had given your most precious possession of all. You had given her your soul.

I unlocked the door then and let my sister in, hearing her yell of delight as Mum and Ros ran up the stairs.

There is not much more to tell. That evening I went for a solitary walk along the shore. The sand was strewn with debris, for there had been a wind and a very high tide the night before. I saw just how high when I reached the fisherman's cottage. The ancient door was splintered and broken and the surging sea had swept away all but a few remnants of the shell walls. The battered kettle hung comically on a piece of driftwood. The silence was like the beginning of the world. I knew then that he had really gone, and what I had to do. I walked back home and behind me the advancing tide wiped away my footsteps. Prophets leave no footprints in the sand.

My future could be put off no longer. When I got inside I telephoned Antony Beaton. It was time for the world to know that Mr Paterson had answered his challenge, and won.

That's how it was, Mr Paterson, and if you are wondering what happened afterwards, I shall set it down here.

Ros won the scholarship to music school and became a famous violinist. The music took her away from us, but I am sure she is happy in her enchanted land. The gods can deny her nothing.

Minnie – you may not like this – Minnie became a television star and has all the excitement even she can handle. She is much loved, for you taught her how to live always in the sun and not to fear the dark beyond. Her light shines like a fire before the watching eyes.

Mum still lives in the old house. She has no need to stay. I could buy her a mansion. But then, as she says, my father would not be there.

And myself? Now you are asking, and I will tell you with my heart.

My photograph of the monster blazed like a comet across an astonished world and in its glittering wake I followed. The image flashed swift as Ariel on countless million screens, and almost in an instant I was rich beyond my dreams, as the legendary king. Free to do anything or nothing, the whole world my kingdom.

Yet I cannot rest. Now I chronicle the earth. Where there is war and grief I go, where there is fire and death, stillness and peace, I am there also. No place is too remote for my camera's eye. I have learnt every skill. There is no angle, no subject I will not attempt. Who has not seen my *Dying Soldier* or my *Little Dancing Child*? They tell me I am the greatest photographer in the world, as once I dreamed they would.

Clever, clever, Mr Paterson; we thought we were helping you, but all the time it was the other way around.

Oh yes, they tell me I am the greatest photographer in the world, but still they are deceived. And I am burdened with their admiration, deaf to their applause. You see, I have not yet their souls and it is their souls I seek. But I know that one day it shall be as it once was, long ago at the Loch's edge. For I have not forgotten the old gods or the pathways to the forest or that mankind is born with a dream. And sometimes beside some foreign sea I fancy I hear the voice of the shell and the sound of it fills my empty heart.